CASE STUDIES IN
CULTURAL ANTHROPOLOGY

GENERAL EDITORS
George and Louise Spindler
STANFORD UNIVERSITY

THE MAPUCHE INDIANS OF CHILE

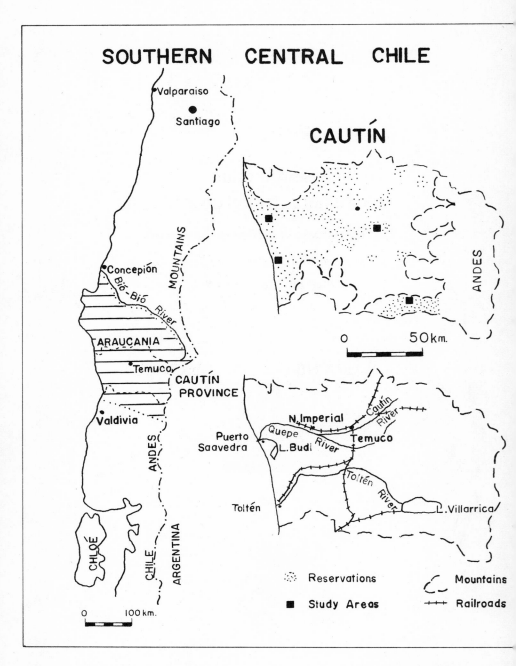

Area in Chile where the Mapuche Indians dwell. At left, Cautín Province, the location of their reservations; at right, two close-ups of the Province.

THE MAPUCHE INDIANS
OF CHILE

By

LOUIS C. FARON

State University of New York at Stony Brook

HOLT, RINEHART AND WINSTON

NEW YORK   CHICAGO   SAN FRANCISCO   ATLANTA
DALLAS   MONTREAL   TORONTO   LONDON

Picture on cover: Mapuche shaman holding kultrun, drumstick, and gourd rattle next to her rewe, a carved effigy pole of sacred significance. The diagram on the drum is the Mapuche representation of the universe.

Library of Congress Catalog Card Number: 68–22733
03–069870–7
Printed in the United States of America
90123   3   98765432

To my children, Amy and Kenneth

Foreword

About the Series

These case studies in cultural anthropology are designed to bring to students in the social sciences insights into the richness and complexity of human life as it is lived in different ways and in different places. They are written by men and women who have lived in the societies they write about, and who are professionally trained as observers and interpreters of human behavior. The authors are also teachers, and in writing their books they have kept the students who will read them foremost in their minds. It is our belief that when one gains an understanding of ways of life very different from one's own, abstractions and generalizations about social structure, cultural values, subsistence techniques, and other universal categories of human social behavior become meaningful.

About the Author

Louis C. Faron is Professor of Anthropology in the State University of New York at Stony Brook, Long Island, N.Y. Dr. Faron received the B.A. and Ph.D. from Columbia University. He has done field work among the Mapuche Indians of Chile (1952–1954), the ethnically complex population of the central coast of Peru (1957–1959), the Choco of Panama (summer 1960), and the Otomi of Mexico (1961, 1962, 1963–1964). His publications include *Native Peoples of South America* (co-authored with Julian H. Steward), 1959; *Mapuche Social Structure*, 1961; *Hawks of the Sun*, 1964; and articles.

About the Book

Dr. Faron has presented us with a case study of a culture that, although subject to great pressure from alien forces, has managed to retain significant traditional characteristics despite centuries of contact and conquest. One of the features of this study is the detailing of the conflict between the forces for change and those for stability. Within the framework of this struggle, the complex relations between the Mapuche and the Chileans (the alien force), and the adaptation of the Mapuche to their contemporary economic, political, and social environment are emphasized. In his description of Mapuche society, Dr. Faron provides us with an especially valuable analysis of the interrelationships among descent groupings, residence patterns, courtship, marriage, and domestic life. Thanks to the clarity of this analysis, these parts of the whole can be seen as a functioning system.

In his description of Mapuche culture, Dr. Faron gives us a vivid picture of the relationship of the Mapuche to the supernatural forces that they believe to be acting upon them and the ways in which these supernatural forces are propitiated and manipulated. The continuity of Mapuche life is revealed in both the patterns of belief that affect the world view of the people and the patterns for behavior that influence their solution to the everyday problems of domestic life, marriage, and making a living. This continuity is seen within the framework of adaptation to external forces.

GEORGE AND LOUISE SPINDLER
General Editors

Phlox, Wisconsin
April 1968

Preview: The Changing Culture and Society

Cultural and social change is an ongoing phenomenon that works in two ways: cultural ideologies influence social institutions, and social institutions, in turn, influence ideologies. These processes, anthropologists believe, are as old as human society.

What attracts today's anthropologists is the rate and degree of this change, especially in those societies that have felt the impact of Western civilization. Since the age of exploration Western technology, politics, economics, and even religion have increasingly brought about radical social change in non-Western societies, whether they have been caught up in its main currents or merely its eddies.

Little attention, however, has been focused on those societies, such as the Mapuche, which have been similarly exposed to European influence—sometimes in its most militant form—but which, for reasons to be shown, have managed for centuries to resist absorption or extinction. The Mapuche Indians, therefore, hold a twofold interest for anthropologists. They are of intrinsic ethnographic interest as a patrilineal society to be described and analyzed, and they are of theoretical interest as a setting in which the interplay of the external forces of change and the internal ones of constancy can be gauged.

The Mapuche, as all people do, organize their life according to traditional sets of beliefs and values. But their neighbors, the Chileans, have since conquest times attempted to alter Mapuche institutions and impose European-derived values on them both through military conquest and by means of social and economic programs. The former attempt met with failure, but the latter has had more success.

The socioeconomic reforms began in 1884 with the implementation of the Chilean government's reservation programs. This date marks the beginning of the modern era for the Mapuche, during which time the most notable changes in their social life took place. Basically, the change involved giving up warfare with the Chileans and becoming agriculturalists. In doing this, they borrowed heavily ideas and technology from their former opponents. Important social and economic changes occurred. Agriculture and animal-raising flourished. The chieftainship became strongly established. In addition, the Mapuche witnessed the perpetuation of extended-family life over several generations; localized patrilineal descent groups grew in size and importance; a rigid system of matrilateral marriage developed; death and fertility rituals became larger and more regularized. All the while, the Mapuche were gradually becoming more involved in the Chilean market economy and politics.

In other ways, however, the Mapuche culture has remained the same. Only negligible change, for instance, has occurred in ritual life and in religion. The

Mapuche also continue to speak Araucanian, their traditional tongue, and although bilingualism is increasing, they still think in Araucanian. Each new generation is thus socialized in the traditional framework of language and values. The reservation system is an especially important factor in preserving their culture. Although diminishing in numbers and area while the population is increasing, the reservations provide an ambience in which Mapuche social institutions can survive and adjust to changing conditions. All of these factors are responsible for maintaining their very conservative culture. Institutional modifications that do occur, thus take place within a framework of tradition.

But mounting pressure portends difficult times for the Mapuche. The legal abolition of reservations was passed by the National Congress of Chile in 1962, and many consider this to be the death-knell for their society. Any current reservation laws have as their primary aim the absorption of the Mapuche into Chilean society.

The Mapuche people, however, have withstood many threats to its existence before and may withstand even the policy of forced abandonment of reservation life. Of central importance to their survival, of course, is their economy. Its viability, and therefore the Mapuche viability, will depend on its ability to respond to the changing environment.

Ultimately though, it will be up to the Mapuche people themselves to find new ways to maintain their unique culture. To accomplish this, they will have to learn the art of adjusting to external exigencies—in this case, Chilean social forces— while at the same time learning how to preserve their traditional values and institutions. The task will not be easy, but the quarter of a million Mapuche Indians will at least give poignancy to the effort.

Louis Faron

Stony Brook, L.I.
April 1968

Contents

1

Studying the Mapuche

Introduction

THIS CASE STUDY attempts to give a concise but well-rounded account of the social life and customary beliefs of a South American Indian population called the Mapuche (see p. ii). The Mapuche live on small reservations in agricultural homesteads in Chile where they raise wheat, potatoes, and other crops, as well as some cattle, a few horses, and many sheep. They have resisted white settlement of their homeland for more than 300 years, and although their culture has undergone changes, the Mapuche have continued to preserve many of their traditional beliefs and social institutions. This cultural conservatism, coupled with a large and growing population, has for many years posed a considerable problem of assimilation for the Chilean government. This is their situation, and our starting point.

The Land and the People

The Mapuche (pronounced ma*pooché*) are a numerous people. The latest estimates of the population that live on reservations range between 250,000 and 300,000. Most of these reservations are in the rolling Central Valley south of the Bio-Bio River, which is now an almost treeless agricultural zone but which was once heavily forested with deciduous trees, such as oak. The trees have been cut down in the process of town-building and the general extension of farmland, due to the fact that the territory is still being colonized by whites.

Reservations are also found along the Pacific Ocean, west of the coastal range of low-lying mountains, and in the Andean foothills. The coastal zone and the Andean area are still rather heavily timbered in several regions, although the timber industry continues to eat into these natural resources without replenishing them by means of an effective reforestation program.

From the Central Valley and even from favored parts of the coast, one is able, on clear days, to see the impressive string of snow capped volcanoes that tower above the Andean range. Some of these erupt violently causing great loss of life and immeasurable property damage, and, in addition, creating havoc and fear among the Mapuche. When the latter happens, they stage ceremonies to propitiate the ancestral spirits and the pantheon of deities that watch over them. Human sacrifice has even been reported in Chilean newspapers during such periods of social stress.

Although the Central Valley has some of the best wheatland in Chile, erosion from wind and rain and lack of proper fertilization serve to impair its productivity. The soil is made up of alluvial glacial deposits and some volcanic ash, and is smooth and easily workable. It turns to soupy mud in the rainy winter months and dries to fine dust in summer.

This zone is favored by cool, dry summers and a winter rainfall of between eighty and 100 inches. Temperatures rarely drop below freezing along the coast and in the Central Valley, but at times there are heavy snows in the Andean uplands during the winter months of July and August. Thin ice appears on puddles but the ground is never frozen to a depth injurious to the germination of winter wheat. Temperature readings taken over several decades indicate a mean of approximately 65°F for the summer season and fifty degrees for the winter months.

The Mapuche live in clusters of households on the reservations on or near their fields, which they cultivate on a family basis. Each reservation is a political unit but the households are set up in whatever place the owner considers most favorable to his needs. The clusters are not nucleated into hamlets or towns, nor are there any physical aspects which might suggest a village or town organization— no streets, no line-arrangement of houses, no central plaza, with market place, church, and official buildings. In short, there is nothing Spanish about the reservations' physical appearance, despite centuries of effort on the part of whites to induce the Mapuche to forsake traditional residential patterns for those more congenial to the Europeans who invaded their territory.

Mapuche live in houses which combine the aboriginal with the centuries of Western influence. There are some pole and thatch houses which fit every description of sixteenth-century Spanish accounts. There are also a few houses with modern wooden frame construction and corrugated iron roof. The vast majority, however, are more traditional than modern. They tend to be rectangular and have rough-hewn plank walls, are windowless, and have one door which is set on oxhide strap hinges. The roof is gently peaked and made of thin logs which are strapped in place and covered with a thick layer of thatch. Some of the houses, more than a half century old, are covered with several layers of thatch, and the insides have been darkened by a thick layer of soot from the perpetually smoking hearth fire. In some cases the thatched eaves come down to within a few feet of the ground, which in the winter afford a second wall of protection from the harsh winds and rain, and in the summer provide welcome shade.

The Mapuche understand our phrase, "A man's home is his castle." They very likely spend more than half their waking hours indoors or a stone's throw from their house. If they wish, they may isolate themselves from neighbors and visitors by staying behind their substantial walls and ground-hugging eaves. Their pack of dogs is able to hold any visitor at bay if the family wishes privacy. Inside the house, the husband and wife, usually seated by the seemingly never-extinguished open fire, decide whether or not to admit the caller. If they wish to ignore him, the dogs are used to discourage his approach; if he is deemed welcome, someone goes out to control the dogs or else simply whistles them off from the shadow of the doorway.

In physical appearance the Mapuche are Mongoloid and easily distinguished from the Caucazoid Chilean and European immigrants who live in the frontier zone. The Mapuche are also easily distinguished from their white neighbors by their dress, their language, and, more subtly, by their different habits of walking, sitting, and so on. Their way of dressing is distinctive, especially women's dress. Women favor traditional clothing, consisting mainly of a homemade wraparound

Mapuche weaver with husband and children, dressed in their finest Western clothing.

which covers them from shoulders to ankles and which is fastened by homemade pins of beaten silver coins. They are fond of traditional jewelry, of which there are several kinds, including necklaces, breast pins, breast plates, earrings, and silver beads plaited into their hair. Modern dresses, aprons, and shoes are also part of women's clothing. The calico dresses and aprons are worn on the reservation, day in and day out, in the ordinary course of activities. The traditional clothing, which is much more costly and more highly valued, is saved for ceremonial events or trips to town. Shoes are worn to town and, sometimes, for greater warmth during the winter months.

Men's clothing, for the most part, is a tattered version of Western dress. Like the women, shoes are seldom worn on the reservation but almost always in town. The only traditional attire worn by the men is the homemade woolen belt which wraps around their waist several times clearly marking them as Mapuche.

Going about the Study

How might an anthropologist go about studying a people such as the Mapuche, a population of upwards of a quarter of a million Indians, living on more than 2000 reservations and occupying an area about the size of the state of Delaware? With that many people spread over such a large area, the study of only one or two reservations might not reveal important social and cultural differences. A main problem, therefore, was to achieve a representative cross-check of the Mapuche.

The Mapuche have been described by soldiers, missionaries, travellers, geographers, and even anthropologists, at different times in the past. These descriptions have been written from many different points of view, and emphasize different aspects of Mapuche life. It is not easy to tell whether the differences are due to different regional adaptations or whether they represent historical changes which have taken place, or some combination of both. This is so because almost none of the historical accounts were made on observations of the same regional populations, but come from here and there throughout Mapucheland at different times in the past. Careful checking of historical sources against contemporary findings helps unravel some of the difficulties.

The area occupied by the Mapuche now and in the past falls into three well-defined geographical zones, with each one having different climates: the coastal strip, the Central Valley, and the Andean uplands. I studied clusters of reservations in each of these zones, believing that if significant cultural and social differences existed among the Mapuche they would be revealed through regional comparisons. The study attempted to discover if there were special ways in which the Mapuche adapted their lives to gaining a livelihood under significantly different environments. Although the results show now that differences among the Mapuche are insignificant from one region to another, east to west or north to south, only the regional studies and the criss-cross survey technique brought the findings to light.

Intensive studies were made near Temuco, Toltén, and Villarrica, in that order. They were all made in the same general way: five months were spent near Temuco, five around Toltén, and two months living south of Villarrica. Survey trips were made, for the most part, in the last few months of fieldwork.

A practical problem in studying the Mapuche was in just gaining access to them. My wife and I arrived in Santiago with a few letters of introduction which opened scientific and political doors in the capital. An interview was almost immediately obtained with a high government official who was a reservation-born Mapuche. He had studied at an Anglican mission school, gone through the Chilean higher educational system and, finally, achieved the highest civil post ever attained by a Mapuche.

This contact, however, for political reasons which I did not understand at the time, was unfavorable. It resulted in word being sent to Mapuche political leaders in Temuco to take delaying action against us and to discourage us from living on the reservations. As it turned out, I was squarely in the middle of Mapuche factionalism.

Fortunately, assistance soon came from another faction which made arrangements for my wife and me to live with a Mapuche family on a reservation about twelve miles outside of Temuco. This was Alonqueo's family and community, with whom we spent our first five months in Mapucheland. Alonqueo's reservation was riven by factionalism, as are many others, and we were immediately plunged into Mapuche politics on a very local and very uncomfortable level. We were judged as having taken sides in an issue of which we then knew almost nothing, and we were even accused of being witches by a few members of the opposing faction. This did not make fieldwork easy, although it added unexpected spice. Witchcraft and politics made a strange mixture, but we were to discover that considerations of witchcraft permeate Mapuche thinking on many subjects, and we often heard the saying: "Each house has its witch."

When we were ready to move to a second region of intensive study, contacts were established through Mapuche who had befriended us during the first phase of study. In accordance with Mapuche etiquette, our departure was formalized by a banquet given by our hosts, which involved a good deal of drinking, maudlin farewells, and tears. Some members of the opposition faction failed to attend the send-off, however.

Our second home-base reservation was at the house of Huenchemil, a chief who lived near the town of Toltén. Until meeting Huenchemil, our stay on the reservations had cost us next to nothing, except for small purchases of wine, canned beef, and cigarettes for ourselves and our hosts. Neither rent nor money was paid to informants, although payment was offered at first. Nor did Huenchemil actually charge us rent or board. However, he immediately apologized for not having a window in his house and within two weeks a Chilean carpenter came out from town to install a frame window with glass panes. This was at my expense.

The move to our third home-base reservation was arranged by Protestant missionaries we knew, some of whom had lived for thirty years among the Mapuche. We went to live with a Mapuche convert named Luís Nahualpan, who lived on a reservation in the mountainous region south of Lake Villarrica. He was a local preacher who also rode circuit[1] as a nonordained representative of the evangelical mission based in Temuco. In his house I said Grace in Spanish for the first time and learned a simple prayer which he had translated into Araucanian. I also learned that in the past twenty years of missionary work in Luís' region, made up of about fifteen reservations, the Protestant group had made fewer than a dozen converts and that Mapuche religious beliefs are tenaciously maintained. As noted before, human sacrifice is still said to occur in times of great general calamity.

In each of the three regions where intensive work was done (Temuco, Toltén, Villarrica), the study began on the reservation on which we lived, actually in our host's house. Then the study was extended to adjacent reservations. In time, certain research leads would be followed across many reservation boundaries. Thus, intensive study areas in each of the three regions may be described as made up of a home-base reservation, on which we lived, and clusters of reservations around it.

The various aspects of Mapuche life that were studied are clearly enough indicated in the Table of Contents and need not be repeated here. It is worth noting, however, that there are two main areas of inquiry which provide excellent starting points for studying the Mapuche: farming and kinship. Farming is what they live by and kinship is what they organize most of their thinking and activities around. These are good starting points, not only because they are of vital interest to the Mapuche but because the Mapuche are quite willing to talk, even to outsiders, about agricultural and kinship organization.

Usually, as the investigations took us from a base reservation to peripheral ones, the inquiries became more specialized and dealt with narrowly defined problems of social organization and cultural values. Do people think and act the same way from one household to another, from one reservation to another? How do members of one reservation interact with and feel about those of another? These questions, of course, may be infinitely refined by phrasing them in different contexts, such as domestic life, marriage practices, political life, religious activities, economic relationships, and so forth. In some instances, certain lines of inquiry were followed to upwards of fifty reservations surrounding the one on which we lived.

Since an anthropologist must try to absorb strange sights and ideas, this kind of coverage alerts one to similarities and differences in many features of Mapuche life no matter what specific clue one is tracking down. Back on the home-base reservation, new impressions could be checked out with friendly informants, and the ideas of all informants checked out against each other from one region to the next.

The intensive studies began in a rather conventional manner. On our arrival, our hosts would assign us a place in one corner of the house to sleep and store our gear. Then they would tactfully inspect us and our belongings, asking where we came from, why we were there, and what this and that object among our possessions was called, how it was used, and so forth. The persons who spoke only

---

[1] One who travels around a large "parrish," traditionally on horseback.

Araucanian would ask us questions through a household member who also spoke Spanish, and, thus, our translator was selected for us. We also asked the names of persons and objects, how the persons were related and how the objects were used. Thus, the study was started.

The Mapuche were always told that we were there to study their language and customs. Even though we never learned Araucanian well, most Mapuche seemed very pleased with our efforts, seldom failing to contrast us with Chileans who did not take the trouble to learn it at all. Inability to grasp their language rapidly did not pose a disadvantage, as feared it might, since it drew from informants repeated answers to our questions, until it became clear, just by repetition, what was sought.

In the very beginning of fieldwork, linguistic hurdles were, however, the hardest to get over. The best way the author found to understand the Mapuche and have them understand us was to limit the subject of conversation and establish a firm basis of discussion before branching out to more general topics. The easiest way to do this was to record single words—write them down in a book—and have our hosts define them for us in Araucanian. Later, I would ask one of the Spanish speakers to translate Araucanian words we did not know.

Anthropologists almost always collect information about genealogical relationships and make lists of the kinship terms used to designate relatives. This traditional procedure provides much information about human relationships in a very short time, and the genealogical information, along with the kinship terminology, provide a solid framework in which to understand most aspects of social organization and related cultural values. Fortunately, Mapuche love to talk about their relatives. Many times it was found that a chance question of ours would trigger a discussion of kinship behavior among our informants which surpassed anything hoped for, and involved political, religious, and economic aspects of kinship rights and obligations.

Obtaining genealogical information was tantamount to beginning a house-to-house census on the reservation itself. The follow-up always involved visits to each house on the reservation, during which additional vital statistics were obtained. Drawing a map of the reservation in the course of taking a census, made it possible to locate all the households thereon, to determine the kinship relationships among them, and to discover the boundaries of the community. This kind of investigation also enabled us to discover which households provided the tastiest meals and harboured the least ferocious pack of dogs. These were the houses most of the time was spent in.

Besides the Mapuche themselves, there is another excellent source of information about their way of life: historical records. In addition to books about the Mapuche, there is the archive of registry records which contains maps of most reservations founded between 1884 and 1912. These records also have house-by-house listings of inhabitants of that period, remarks about how these people were related, and other choice bits of information. It is no trick at all to link such recent historical data to contemporary reservation life through the detailed discussion of family trees, patrilineal lines of descent, subsequent births, deaths, marriages, and so forth. Even the mere mapping of today's reservations shows how many houses have been built since 1884 and, therefore, shows something of the changes which have taken place in family growth, household composition, residential patterns, and many other important and related matters.

The several research techniques that have been singled out for mention are only preliminary ways of establishing the general social and cultural framework within which the Mapuche live. While they are essential beginnings, they are no substitute for long conversations with Mapuche informants, day in and day out, under all sorts of circumstances.

Principal Informants

Anthropologists usually collect information from as many people as possible, cross-checking information and building up a model of the life-ways of the society they are studying. Some informants, however, being more talkative, knowledgeable, friendlier, are better than others. One man may be an excellent source of agricultural information, another man an expert genealogist, a woman the best informant about Mapuche sex life, love magic, and so on. Among my best general informants are those already mentioned: Alonqueo, Huenchemil, and Luís Nahualpan.

Alonqueo was twenty three years old when we first met him in 1952. He was planning to marry his sweetheart from another reservation, and we were guests at his wedding before we left Mapucheland. Alonqueo was toothless, exceptionally tall (5 ft. 10 in.) and, unexceptionally, tubercular. I received news of his death in 1960.

Huenchemil was forty five years old, the father of three children, and physically fit. He had succeeded to his father's status as chief of the reservation, after his father's death, some years before we arrived in Chile. Furthermore, Huenchemil was appointed *regidor* (minor civil official of the Chilean town of Toltén), during our stay on his reservation. I was told that he was the first Mapuche to receive this honor. Huenchemil was fully bilingual in Araucanian and Spanish, while Alonqueo had a good deal of difficulty with Spanish.

Luís Nahualpan was thirty years old, unmarried, slightly tubercular, and lived with his widowed mother and separated sister. His mother bemoaned Luís' conversion to Christianity; his sister seemed indifferent to it. Luís was fully bilingual and was also able to read Spanish well, and to explain the Bible in both Spanish and Araucanian.

It must be stated here that all of the Mapuche who welcomed my wife and me into their houses were, to a certain degree, unusual, simply because they were willing to have us in their homes for several months. While this probably introduced a measure of bias into the impressions of the Mapuche, our study tried to counteract it by being continually aware of the danger of bias and by gathering information from as wide a range of informants as possible.

2

Warfare and Peace

MOST OF WHAT IS KNOWN about the Mapuche past is closely related to their hostilities with whites and their eventual pacification.

Mapuche means "people of the land" (mapu: land; che: people) and is often used synonymously by anthropologists with the word *Araucanian.* Technically, Araucanian refers to a much larger, partly extinct, and geographically more extensive population, and one which was culturally more heterogeneous than are the contemporary, reservation-dwelling Mapuche. Araucanian is also the name given to the language spoken by the Mapuche, and to mutually intelligible dialects used to the north and south of them. Araucanian belongs to the Andean subfamily of the Andean-Equatorial language family, which is widespread in South America.

To Spaniards and, after Independence (1810), to Chilean nationals, the word Mapuche suggested hostile Indian and was used to refer to all Araucanians who resisted conquest and were, therefore, considered fair game for slaving raids and other forms of human degradation, such as enforced labor on ranches and in gold mining, mutilation of recalcitrants (for example, cutting leg tendons to make escape difficult, cutting off male genitals), and subjecting Mapuche women to concubinage. In today's Chilean elementary school textbooks, however, Mapuche militarism receives qualified praise, and culture heroes, such as Lautaro and Caupaulican are described as valiant and astute leaders. Statues have even been raised to their memory here and there in Chilean cities. Nevertheless, the contemporary reservation Mapuche are disparaged. Their problems are sloughed off, and their basic needs are ignored. "Lauto" and "Caupo," as the two military heroes are commonly called, have become cigar-store Indians.

What does being "of the land" mean to the Mapuche homesteader? What are the sorrows and joys attached to having been "of the land" since time immemorial? Part of the answer to these questions may be glimpsed in the highly selective account of warfare and pacification which follows. The Mapuche know something of their early history from legends and from school books and newspaper articles which some of them have read. This knowledge is spread, even if imperfectly, over all Mapucheland by word of mouth in the form of stories and tales. The Mapuche know much more about their more recent history, chiefly from accounts of the founding of reservations being passed down orally from one generation to the next.

Military Resistance to Conquest

Inca forces were unable to conquer the Mapuche. Spanish armies fared no better. After Chile acquired independence from Spain, its own troops also tried. They too were no more successful against the Mapuche than the Spanish troops had been, that is, until 1882. Since 1882, the Mapuche have been living at peace with the whites.

In 1540 Pedro de Valdivia arrived in Chile with a handful of troops, established Santiago as a military outpost of Peru, and worked at bringing the Picunche Araucanians to heel. The Picunche (picun: north), although resisting and causing great damage to the Spaniards for a time, were subjugated rather rapidly and forced to work for their new masters placer-mining gold and raising crops and cattle on Spanish estates. The Picunche were absorbed as mestizos into colonial society during the first century of the conquest period. The conquest of the Picunche was, however, a bitter victory for the Spaniards: their small population did not provide the manpower the Spaniards needed. Because of this, Valdivia pushed into Mapucheland south of the Bio-Bio River, in an attempt to harness Mapuche manpower and exploit the resources of their country. The Picunche are long gone and almost forgotten. The Mapuche are still a force to contend with.

Valdivia's expeditions into Mapucheland in the middle of the sixteenth century appeared to be successful, and within a short time he established seven outposts. At this time it is conservatively estimated that the Mapuche population was 500,000, an overwhelming superiority of numbers against the Spaniards.

With the founding of each new settlement, Valdivia made huge grants of Indians to his officers. One of his captains received 30,000 Indians, others from 8 to 12,000 each. The Spaniards put as many Mapuche as they could to panning gold in the rivers. Chroniclers tell of the harsh conditions suffered by the Indians. Hostilities soon broke out and all mining operations were disrupted. The towns and forts the Spaniards had built were razed, many settlers were killed, some were evacuated by boat and returned to Santiago. Although some of these settlements were later rebuilt, they never again prospered.

Because of their hostility, the Mapuche were considered fair game for slaving parties during the next centuries. Nevertheless, the Mapuche managed to keep the Spaniards out of their heartland and retained most of their ancestral territory for the next three hundred years. The Mapuche staged several major uprisings and waged continual guerrilla warfare against the Spaniards. One time they even penetrated Spanish-held territory to the very gates of Santiago, but were driven back south of the Bio-Bio River.

The aggressive resistance of the Mapuche caused the Spaniards great apprehension and cost the Crown a good deal of money for supplies and troops which had to be sent to save Chile, its colony. Not only did the Spaniards fail to conquer the Mapuche, they had to devise an effective, and expensive, means of preventing their being overrun by them.

It was not until toward the end of the nineteenth century that there was any deep penetration of Mapucheland. Raids continued, however, and captives were taken by both sides. Several epidemics swept Mapucheland and untold thousands died by contracting European diseases to which they had no immunity. Many Mapuche migrated across the Andes into Argentina. By the end of the nineteenth century, Mapuche population had probably been reduced to no more than 100,000.

The Picunche had long since been absorbed as mestizos into colonial society north of the Bio-Bio River. To the south of the city of Valdivia there are still remnants of a once larger population called Huilliche (huilli: south) who represent the southernmost branch of Araucanians. Relatively few Huilliche live on reservations. Most have been absorbed into the mestizo element of Chilean society since the second half of the nineteenth century and are known by several different local names. The only viable segment of Araucanian society is that of the Mapuche, preserved largely as a result of the protection afforded by the reservation system begun in 1884, and geographically intermediate to the now-extinct Picunche and the vanishing Huilliche.

Although the Mapuche maintained their independence until the latter part of the nineteenth century, a good deal of the price of independence was paid in the form of social upheaval and population dispersal. The long colonial era had been one of continual guerrilla skirmishing, occasional general uprisings, and periodic loss of territory.

Pacification

When Chile secured independence from Spain in 1818 there appeared to be an awakening of national interest in the further colonization of Mapucheland. The new government expressed interest in protecting the Mapuche from the hardships of increased contact with Chilean settlers through legislation designed to prevent the unauthorized acquisition of Indian land. The government was, nevertheless, interested in having the frontier zone transformed into one of productive small farms, and had no intention of allowing the Mapuche to hold all the land they claimed as their own. Safeguards were also established against speculation in land, which might have lead to the formation of huge Chilean estates. Official policy and legal precautions were consistent with the two-fold purpose of assuring the Mapuche adequate land and, at the same time, opening up some of the area to small farmers.

Also contained in the post-independence legislation was a hope, later made very explicit, that the Mapuche would eventually abandon their traditional way of life and seek employment on Chilean farms and in the cities and towns of the future. The new national government envisioned the eventual use of both Mapuche land and labor, as other governments had in the past. To a great extent this policy, although revamped periodically since its initiation, has been unsuccessful. Even though the Mapuche have lost a good deal of their land to colonists, they have not been easily transformed into the rural and urban working class envisioned by the Chilean government and/or landed class.

By the middle of the nineteenth century white colonization had received a new impulse from European immigration. New encroachments on Mapuche territory aroused them and resulted in their intensification of guerrilla activity. The Chilean government attempted to foster colonization by establishing the reservation policy of 1866. Under its terms, Mapuche leaders were allowed to apply for large grants of reservation land for themselves and their followers. At the same time, the law provided a mechanism for the gradual dissolution (*división*) of the reservation communities it created. Meanwhile, all unclaimed land was to be sold to white settlers.

It was during this period that the Huilliche, subjected to large-scale settlement of their land by German immigrants, began to lose control of their traditional way of life. The Mapuche, however, seemed to lose little or none of their former vigor.

After 1866 tremendous pressure was exerted against the Mapuche by white colonists. Huge tracts of land were taken from them along the Bio-Bio River, along the coast south of Concepción, and in a vast area north and south of the town of Valdivia. The Mapuche responded, as they had in the past, by staging a major rebellion, from 1869–1870, in which they were defeated and their population further dispersed and socially disrupted. Peace ensued for less than a decade. The final great Mapuche revolt came in 1880 and lasted about two years. Again, peace was established, but this time the military power and political autonomy of the Mapuche were lost. Great population flux characterized the decade or so after 1884, during the establishment of the present reservation system. The exodus to Argentina assumed proportions greater than ever before. The Mapuche who remained in Chile, although restive under defeat and a harsh peace, were willing to accept the protection of the reservation system, the basis for present-day Mapuche society.

Since that time the population has increased greatly. Aside from the quarter million or so Mapuche who live on reservations, there are unknown thousands living and working in Chilean towns and cities, on Chilean farms, and in the national army and police force. But the geographical spread of the reservations, despite territorial losses and shifts in population, still lies within the aboriginal boundaries formed by the Bio-Bio River on the north and the Calle-Calle River in the south.

The heartland of the contemporary Mapuche is formed by Cautín and Malleco provinces, where the majority of reservations are found. As one moves north and south from the heartland to the aboriginal boundaries, the number of reservations diminishes sharply, and the Mapuche population dwindles almost to the point of extinction. In effect, the occupied area has been compressed as a result of white intrusions from the north and the south, during periods of encroachment in the last four centuries. There has been a marked redistribution of both land and population.

It is obvious in looking at the map on page ii that, although there are large blocks of reservations in the heartland, there are also large "blank" areas, and that reservations do not cover the heartland uniformly. For the most part, the blank areas on the map are now occupied by white settlers who began to make serious inroads on the Mapuche stronghold only since the closing decades of the last century. It was around that time, too, after pacification and the establishment of reservations, that towns, roads, and railroads began to be built in Mapuche territory. This was territory over which the Mapuche had been accustomed to roam with relative freedom.

It should not be thought that the blank areas within the heartland were once covered by reservations or settled by permanent Mapuche residential groupings before or after 1884 and, that, therefore, these areas were *wrested* from the reservation-dwelling Indians. This is not the case. Most of the blank area was never accounted for in the reservation system of 1884. Prior to pacification, and under the previous and ineffectual reservation system of 1866, the blank spaces comprised a heavily forested and/or swampy, unoccupied land which, at most, offered a place of retreat for warring bands of Mapuche during periods of peak stress. Most of the redistribution of land and population involved the compression of the Mapuche into their present habitat, driving them from the peripheries of their aboriginal territory. This occurred in several phases from the middle of the sixteenth century to 1884 and, in regard to reservation land specifically, between 1884 and the early 1920s, the number of reservations has remained constant, a phenomenon which reflects a cultural resistance of the latter-day Mapuche, rather than a lessening of the acquisitive attitude of Chilean society.

There is some indication that at the time of the Spaniards' arrival in Chile the Mapuche lived in relatively stable agricultural communities, at least in the most favorable parts of their territory, and that continual skirmishing with the whites put an end to this sedentary life. In any case, it is obvious that fighting with Spanish troops for a couple of centuries served to make the Mapuche highly mobile. Mobility was both a strategy of attack and retreat (as in most guerrilla campaigns) and it is likely that the shifting type of garden cultivation which was practiced by them during the colonial era developed in response to their increasingly mobile way of life.

The reservation system ushered in a period of much greater stability, during which time local groups could remain settled on their agricultural lands for generations. A change to field farming at least correlates with the greater stability, even if it did not actually reinforce it at first. At the same time, military organization withered as garden horticulture became almost entirely woman's work, and men turned their attention to field farming and animal raising. It is simple enough to show that out of the reservation system there developed a pattern of life based largely on membership in patrilineal units; a life in which patrilineal descent groups become fundamental units in Mapuche economics, politics, religion, kinship, and marriage connections, and in other facets of institutionalized, normative behavior.

One-quarter million or more Mapuche, conservative and recalcitrant, continue to pose a great problem of assimilation for the Chilean government. On the regional level of intersocietal relationships, there has long been conflict between white Chileans and reservation-dwelling Mapuche, in many spheres of activity and belief. The Mapuche regard most Chileans with distrust, even suspecting them of being sorcerers. Short of this, Chileans are felt to be unscrupulous merchants and land grabbers who are unjustly protected by Chilean law. Most Chileans regard the Mapuche as intellectually inferior savages. Antagonism is aggravated by the fact that Mapuche reservations occupy some of the best farm land and pasturage in Chile, land which is coveted by white settlers who complain that reservations surround them like a "ring of iron," cutting off their potential expansion.

Merchants and bankers in the towns echo this complaint because most of their profits depend on the agricultural production of the frontier zone. The Chilean government is desirous that the land be exploited by the best agricultural techniques, and regards the Mapuche as a stumbling block to modern farming and larger returns. These attitudes are translated into pressures on Mapuche and Chilean society alike. They are part of the environmental and social adaptations made by both Mapuche and Chilean.

3

Agriculture

MAPUCHE AGRICULTURE has been influenced greatly by contact with Chileans, especially since the beginning of the reservation system and the increase in white colonization of Mapucheland. Prior to pacification, agriculture was woman's work. Rather than extensive farms, the characteristic agricultural unit was a vegetable garden, in which native crops were grown under the care of women and children. Women still cultivate kitchen gardens and tend the family's animals. But men now engage in field-farming European crops, using ox-drawn steel plows, and employing farming techniques learned from Chileans, such as a three-field system of land rotation that is complemented by crop rotation. These are features now characteristic of Mapuche agriculture and considered to be traditional by most Mapuche.

Agricultural Techniques and Goals

The study team arrived in Mapucheland at the beginning of the harvest season and departed the following year at the end of the harvest. The day we took up residence for the first time on a Mapuche reservation, Alonqueo pointed out a parcel of land to us and told us that next year it would be covered by tall-standing wheat. He described in some detail how the land would be prepared, sown, cultivated, and so forth. This was my introduction to Mapuche agriculture, its techniques and goals.

The next year, upon returning to say goodbye to Alonqueo before leaving Chile, we saw that the parcel of land for which he had had such high hopes was covered by a ragged stubble which indicated a very poor crop. Underscoring the failure was the obvious fact that Alonqueo's family, along with many others on the reservation, had lost much weight (up to 25 pounds) during the lean preharvest months. Almost everyone I spoke to complained about the harvest. In spite of this, one could sense the euphoria that accompanies harvest time throughout Mapucheland.

We ate very well during our final week among Alonqueo's people. We dined several times a day on freshly baked bread, pitted with cinders from the ashes of the open fire under which it had been buried. We made decisions, had true alternatives, whether or not to have mutton soup, pork soup, or goose soup, with or without potatoes. We opted for special sauces. We chose spit broiled chops, pork or mutton, for lunch or supper. For breakfast, while they lasted, we were unanimous in selecting broiled livers and kidneys and coagulated blood. As a tried and true friend of Alonqueo's reservation, I was served more sheep's eyes in that final week than I had eaten in the entire year of my residence in Mapucheland. Twice in that week I dined on the supreme delicacy, parboiled lungs of sheep which had been slaughtered in such a way that the lungs were swollen with blood. All that was lacking was mare's meat, a special dish at births, marriages, and deaths.

The Mapuche eat sumptuously in the immediate postharvest season. This is also a time of much visiting, many small fiestas. It is topped off by a round of fertility rites, involving several reservations, during which additional large quantities of food are consumed.

The Mapuche dig deeply into food supplies which, even after a good harvest, are barely sufficient to see them through to the next year. Furthermore, some of the harvest—mainly wheat—is sold for cash or used to repay debts to Chilean businessmen, for the satisfaction of a number of induced needs, such as the purchase of cloth, tobacco, wine, and other commodities which ease life and which may also be necessary to the staging of the forthcoming agricultural ceremonies.

A full larder and enough surplus for cash sales are Mapuche agricultural goals. In most years, however, the Mapuche have to contend with several lean months before the next crops are garnered. How do they meet this problem and what alternatives do they have?

Let us consider for a moment what the Mapuche farmer does *not* do. He does not contour-plow hilly land nor build terraces, as do the more advanced Chilean farmers. If he were conditioned to the custom, contour plowing would be easy enough to accomplish and would help check the terrible erosion which plagues Mapucheland. Terracing with the use of heavy machinery is beyond his means, although Mapuche work gangs could build terraces with traditional equipment. More than being beyond financial or manpower means, terracing is beyond the technological understanding of most Mapuche, and this holds in large measure for contour plowing as well.

A family on Alonqueo's reservation I knew well had a parcel of hillside which abutted on the reservation's ceremonial field. One day, when the two young brothers had begun to plow this field, they were visited by their older half-brother who had come out from Temuco to see how the work was progressing. The latter was a relatively well-educated man, an elementary school teacher highly respected in the region. His younger brothers followed his advice on most matters and were eager to share his opinions. When he saw them plowing up and down hill, he laughed in the manner characteristic of an elder, knowledgeable relative and began a well-taken lecture on the advantages of contour plowing. His brothers shuffled their feet, smiled sheepishly once in a while (a characteristic response) and asked him some questions. Then work stopped and we all went to the house for the evening meal.

A few days later work was resumed on the field; plowing continued to be up and down hill. I did not say a word about this, but the brothers seemed to sense that I wanted some explanation. They told me pretty much the following.

It was easier, they told me, to make even furrows the way they were plowing. Their citified brother seemed to have forgotten that he used to plow in the same manner. They had seen contour-plowed land which had been badly eroded, and were not convinced that contouring worked. Anyway, their wheat would not be washed away, since they were going to use chemical fertilizer. Fertilizer would make the roots grow longer and hold the plants in place. Finally, if they contoured the slope, they would not be able to· plow up as much ground because the curved sweep of their furrows would cut into the ceremonial field at the bottom of the slope. It was unthinkable to cut into sacred ground. Therefore, they would have to stop far short of it. Up and down plowing was the better method for this field.

In the above instance, fertilizer was actually used, but with poor results. The vast majority of Mapuche do not use chemical fertilizer because of its high cost, although they often use manure from the corral in the kitchen gardens. The Mapuche reason that chemical fertilizer is more expensive than a bag of wheat grain, which may be planted or eaten, and that fertilization does not produce uniformly good harvests. Their observation is correct. What they fail to understand, however, is that fertilizer which is misapplied may have little good effect and may even burn the plants. The Mapuche farmer is only dimly aware of the advantages of modern technology and is distrustful of non-Mapuche who encourage its use on the reservations.

Proper rotation of fields and crops would improve Mapuche harvests. The Mapuche have practiced rotation of crops and fields for several decades and say that a three-field rotation of farmland is the ideal solution to their agricultural needs. Nevertheless, the relentless fragmentation of holdings makes it impossible for most Mapuche to set aside part of their land in fallow. Since scarce land is an extreme problem in the Central Valley (where I began work with the Mapuche) one wondered how an agricultural ideal could enjoy such persistence when it was so often disregarded in practice. Later it was discovered that in the more sparsely populated coastal region and in the Andean foothills fields were generally rotated according to the ideal pattern.

Even when the ideal is at least partly observed, and some land is left fallow (unsowed) each year, agricultural yields do not seem to increase much. Some of the reasons for this are that dead fallow is no solution to the problem of impoverished soil. Animals, especially sheep, are allowed to over-graze the fallows, and winter rains and summer winds heavily erode the bare land. The Mapuche do not plant soil restorative crops, such as clover and lupine, which would also serve as pasturage. Even some of the more advanced Chilean farmers are reluctant to take the agronomists' advice to plant clover and lupine, and the Mapuche farmers, therefore, have no example whatever to follow or think about.

Wheat is the main crop in the Central Valley and is also grown on the best, driest land along the coast and in the Andean region. Potatoes are the next most important crop, followed by barley, beans, oats, some linseed, and a little rye. These crops could be rotated so that some would put back into the soil what others take out. In the absence of proper fertilization, however, the results would not be spectacular.

The Mapuche believe that a rotation of crops is useful, but have no firm guideline to follow in planning rotation. They allow essentially nonagricultural considerations to determine what crops they plant each year. One farmer on Luís Nahualpan's reservation told me that he would plant beans in his fallow, since the previous crop had been wheat and he had heard that rotating beans and wheat would improve the richness of the soil. Before he could act on his decision, a neighbor convinced him that barley would be a better crop than beans, as indicated by the fact that a local Chilean farmer was planting barley in several of his fields. Luís suggested that he plant potatoes or *oca*, and offered to lend his plowing discs. This offer was rejected, largely because, as things turned out, our Mapuche farmer went to the Chilean to buy barley seed only to discover that the Chilean had planted wheat instead of barley. On the strength of this, the Mapuche finally sowed wheat.

There are also "supernatural" considerations which affect farming decisions. During agricultural fertility rites the Mapuche pray for good fortune with respect to next year's harvests, animals, and human well-being. They tend to single out one crop for special attention in such ceremonies, very often wheat. When this is done, many Mapuche will abandon all thought about rotating fields and crops to plant their entire holding in wheat (or potatoes or beans, as the case may be). This results in a restriction on crop diversification throughout the locality, which involves many reservations, with all or most of the farmers suffering the same fortunes of weather, plant blight, and so forth. Near famine conditions have resulted from this kind of supernaturally induced monocropping. The forces of evil are then blamed for Mapuche hardship. If, by chance, the harvests are good, it is felt that the fertility ceremony had its intended effect and belief in the ritual is reinforced.

Finally, there are market considerations which influence Mapuche farmers. The crop in greatest demand in wholesale markets throughout Mapucheland is wheat, although almost any other crop raised by the Mapuche is salable in retail markets. Wheat, however, brings the surest returns to the Mapuche farmer. It is also a crop on which he may obtain credit among Chilean businessmen. The ability to transform wheat into credit and goods reinforces the Mapuche preference for wheat growing and thereby serves to curtail large-scale crop diversification on the reservations.

As already discussed, where land is not too scarce, some of it is left fallow for a year or more. Land set aside for producing a crop in any one year is plowed in the fall of the year, ideally several times in a criss-cross pattern. Only winter varieties of wheat are used by the Mapuche, and by most Chileans, and planting takes place in late fall. At planting time the field may receive a final plowing. Often the soil is lightly harrowed after the grain has been broadcast sown. No weeding takes place during the growth cycle. The farmer just sits back and awaits the harvest period.

It has been said that the Mapuche are indifferent farmers. While there may be some truth to this, it seems closer to the truth to say that they are essentially ignorant of alternative methods to improve their farming. The Mapuche feel that a yield of wheat in a ratio of twenty bags harvested for each bag sown is excellent. Such a return is impossible under the conditions I have been describing. A good harvest is gauged at 10:1, but I did not see a single harvest yielding such a high return after the traditional technology had been employed. During the two harvest seasons I was on the reservations, returns were often as low as 3:1. Government agricultural figures for the decades 1930–1939 and 1940–1949 indicate that very low returns of this sort are not uncommon on the reservations. The Mapuche are finding it more and more difficult to subsist at their traditional level of technology.

Traditional Cooperation among Neighbors

There are no adequate descriptions of labor organization for the prereservation period, but after the formation of reservations around the turn of the century, descriptions are fairly complete. Two principal forms of cooperative labor which have a long history in Mapucheland are *mingaco* and *vuelta mano*.

Mingaco implies a fairly large labor gang under the direction of a leader who provides the workers with ample food and drink. The mingaco pattern has undergone some modification over the several generations since the establishment of reservations.

When reservations were mapped and the inhabitants registered by the Chilean government, each registry document contained the name of the "chief" or cacique, his relatives, and nonrelated coresident neighbors. The reservation chief had the authority to control agricultural labor organization, which soon became geared to the cropping cycle that had been introduced along with field-farming European plants, such as wheat. Chief Huenchemil and Alonqueo, a member of a subbranch of a chiefly line, concurred on the general description which follows.

For a generation or more after pacification it was customary for the chief to initiate the several phases of the annual cycle of agricultural events, such as preparation of fields, planting, determination of what to plant and where, and harvesting. He would invite the household heads of his reservation to assemble at his house on a certain day to begin plowing his fields. These men brought whatever equipment and draft animals they owned, and were most often accompanied by their immediate families. The work day was punctuated by drinking wine or the native brew called *chicha* and ended in a rather copious banquet at the chief's expense.

After the chief's land had been prepared there was a round of similar activities in which each household head acted as host, fêted the participants, organized the work, and so on. The round of work ended when all households were accounted for. Because of his high status the chief was invited to all such activities, although he seldom made more than token participation in actual field labor. Even today, the chief is invited to lend his presence to communal labor activities and enjoy the drinking and eating. Alonqueo complained that his great-uncle enjoyed this prestige and that his family, being a subline, was deprived of it. Huenchemil enjoyed this kind of prestige and, after being told him of Alonqueo's case, was not at all sympathetic to Alonqueo.

The main characteristics of this kind of labor are festivity and reciprocity, features which are also apparent in other phases of the agricultural cycle, such as harvesting, threshing, and winnowing, although not always on a reservation-wide basis.

Nowadays, work gangs tend to be smaller than in the past and are usually made up of one's closest kinsmen, say, several brothers, their father, and their father's brother and his sons. As we shall see later, such work units are composed of members of branch lines of larger patrilineal descent groups on the reservations. They are work gangs which engage in the preparation of fields and other activities directly or immediately connected to the production of food crops, both for consumption and sale.

There are still reservation-wide work gangs which unite to clear land, dig or repair canals to drain swamps, repair reservation wagon roads, and undertake operations such as house-building, preparation of the ceremonial field, and so forth. Indeed, some of these enterprises may occasionally involve the cooperation of members of more than one reservation. There also continue to be reservation-wide cooperative labor gangs for working the fields of chiefs and for those of wealthy men (*ulmen*), respect and festivity appearing to be the major inducements for cooperation of this sort.

The other traditional form of labor organization, *vuelta mano*, is one which involves two "parties," either two men by themselves or with the participation of other males of their households. Vuelta mano, which means an exchange of hands, calls for reciprocity between the two men over the years, even for their entire adult lives, and the agreement is not infrequently honored by their sons after their death. The author recorded vuelta mano arrangements which have endured for three generations.

In the vuelta mano agreement, one man provides some agricultural require-ment for his partner, usually labor but also draft animals, or a plow or harrow, and expects his partner to reciprocate labor and needed equipment upon demand. The vuelta mano relationship is always based on kinship; the men are always related. This may be taken as the minimal requirement for agreement. But trust and personal friendship are also necessary for such an arrangement to be made and deemed rewarding for the parties involved.

Kinship, therefore, overlain by friendship, is characteristic of vuelta mano. Friendship is not a necessary element in mingaco, arranged as it usually is by an elder kinsmen who has the acknowledged right to demand cooperation from relatives, or by the chief who enjoys both kinship and political rights with which to command economic loyalty from his coresidents, kinsmen or not.

Cooperation with Chileans

While mingaco and vuelta mano are clearly aboriginal, prereservation institutions, another form of cooperative labor has developed since the beginning of the reservation period again as a response to agricultural needs throughout Mapucheland. This is a half-share system, involving crops or cattle and sheep, arranged between Chilean farmer and reservation-dwelling Mapuche. The Chilean is always desirous of more land, land held by the Mapuche whom he complains surround him like a "ring of iron." By working on a share basis with a Mapuche farmer, and arranging to use the Indian's land, the Chilean is able to break through the ring of iron. He pays half the harvest to his Mapuche partner for the opportunity. This condition is now widespread in Mapucheland.

The Chilean farmer usually initiates the arrangement, visiting one or more reservations near his *fundo* (large farm) and discussing the possibility of using the farm with the Mapuche, whom he has come to know over many years or from a lifetime of residence in the area. The Mapuche farmer is induced to work half-shares with the Chilean for several reasons. Observing the better harvests on the Chilean's land, he admires their tractors, discs, seeding machines, and so forth. He is also often hard put to save enough seed from his previous harvest to make an adequate planting the following year. The astute Chilean farmer is aware of this difficulty. It is in bad years that Mapuche are most willing to enter into such agreements with their Chilean neighbors, years in which they have been forced to grind their seeds into flour or slaughter most of their sheep and breed cows for food. Finally, even if they have to share half the harvest with a Chilean, the half of the harvest which remains at their disposal is greater and sometimes many times greater than that which they could customarily reap alone. The greater return may also be enough for the Mapuche farmer to resolve debts incurred over the previous years.

Since the Chilean provides everything but the land, the Mapuche farmer gains much in this kind of relationship. If animals are involved instead of crops, the Chilean pastures his cattle or sheep on the reservation for one year. When the offspring are born, one half of them go to the Mapuche on whose land they grazed.

Despite the obvious advantages, the Mapuche resent the intrusion of Chileans on the reservations. They do not trust Chileans. They sometimes express feelings of degradation in that they have relinquished all managerial controls to outsiders and thus sense a spiritual failure on their part. This was expressed to me poignantly by a middleaged Mapuche chief living near Toltén. He asked rhetorically, "How could the Mapuche, who worked with a Christian, continue to celebrate the agricultural rites. How could he dispel the forces of evil?" No libations are poured when the halfshared crop is harvested. No ritual, no commensality is observed at the various critical periods of the agricultural cycle. There is none of the traditional joy, no festivity, no obligation to ancestors—nothing. Yet, harvests are better; there is more to eat. Children are not kept away from school because of agricultural chores and they have enough food to take a lunch every day.

4

Descent and Descent Groups

K INSHIP TIES channel almost all important interpersonal relationships
among the Mapuche. Persons who have the most enduring relationships with one another in matters of economic organization, politics,
religion, and marriage, are kinsmen and neighbors. The principal working relationships of a day-to-day kind are those founded on blood ties. The Mapuche do
not define blood ties in the manner of most Western peoples but conceive them
in a framework of patrilineal descent.

Patrilineal Principles and Groupings

The Mapuche are a patrilineally organized people. They trace descent
through their father, father's father, and so on, back to an ancestral male who is
often shrouded in myth and is believed to be the founder of the lineage. Everyone
in Mapuche society is a member by birth of a patrilineal descent group in which
he retains membership throughout his or her life. After death he is considered to
be an ancestral spirit of his patrilineage and is propitiated thereafter by its living
members. In tracing descent patrilineally, men are socially more important than
women and male spirits are remembered longer and are more highly revered after
death than those of females. This, however, does not mean that women are
unimportant in Mapuche society.

Lineages are made up of a varying but usually large number of persons who
were born on the same reservation. Alonqueo's lineage, for example, numbered
approximately 250 living persons, that of his mother slightly more. Some lineages
are much smaller than Alonqueo's and some are considerably larger. As mentioned,
there are about 2,200 reservations in Mapucheland each of which has from one to
several patrilineal descent groups.

The Mapuche have been governed by patrilineal principles of descent,
inheritance, and succession for centuries, as indicated by accounts of their way of

life in early Spanish chronicles. The cultural principles have remained remarkably constant during the centuries but there has been significant modification in the social organization, especially since the formation of reservations in the closing years of the nineteenth century. Large, localized, corporate patrilineal descent groups have gradually developed on the reservations and are different from the household or multihousehold organizations (also patrilineally organized) which existed in prereservation times.

A number of forces have contributed to these organizational changes and have at the same time worked for the persistence of patrilineality. Pacification is one of these, settlement on reservations with fixed boundaries is a complementary one, new agricultural goals and techniques is a third. A fourth major force was the alteration in the authority structure of the Mapuche by the creation of more than 3,000 peacetime chiefs who controlled agricultural land.

The *lonko* (head), formerly only a kinship elder of a patrilineal extended-family, became chief of the reservation which Chilean surveyors mapped out around his holdings. He was selected by Chilean officials and given chiefly status over related households and, perhaps more importantly, over those few nonrelated households which were also registered on most reservations during the beginning years of the reservation period. Since the beginning of the reservation era the chief has enjoyed previously unknown authority in the organization of political, economic, religious, and marriage arrangements.

Mapuche population has increased since the beginning of the reservation period from an estimated 100,000 to its present 250,000 or more. This population is pressing on scarce reservation land. A desire to live the Mapuche way of life and a lack of alternatives to abandon it successfully have resulted in the formation of patrilineages which are broad-based and which have a generational depth beyond anything known to the Mapuche during the warring prereservation era. Most lineages have increased in size and have spawned important sub- or branch-lineages.

Lineages and Sublineages

The following analytic distinctions are helpful in defining Mapuche social relationships which are based on membership in patrilineages. They are not made as sharply by the Mapuche as is done here, although the Araucanian language does conceptualize these categories. There are five lineage units of importance: (1) maximal lineage, (2) lineage group, (3) localized lineage, (4) sublineage, and (5) minimal lineage. These distinctions make it possible to view the totality of blood kinsmen from different angles, according to the kinship activities under scrutiny.

(1) *Maximal lineages* are made up of a body of blood kinsmen who trace descent, usually from four to six generations, back to a common male ancestor who is considered to be the founder of the particular descent line. The maximal lineage incorporates all of the subunits listed above. It comprises both the living and the dead, males and females. The deceased males constitute the agnatic[1] links with the

---

[1] A relative whose relationship is exclusively through patrilineally related males.

founding ancestor and head up branch lineages through which contemporary relationships are figured. In the propitiation of ancestral spirits and in the celebration of agricultural fertility rites and funeral ceremonies, the maximal lineage is a religious unit *par excellence*, with both living and the dead playing complementary roles of a corporate nature.

(2) The *lineage group* is made up of all the living members of the maximal lineage. It is characteristically a nonlocalized social unit, since it includes women of the lineage who have moved off their natal reservation after marriage, in observance of the rule of lineage exogamy and the custom of patrilocal residence (in other words, they move to their husband's natal reservation). Nowadays, there are a number of males who move off the reservation of their birth, for one reason or another, and who are kept track of by their kinsmen. These males may exercise lineage-based rights, however, and they will be propitiated after they die by their heirs and close relatives who have remained on the reservations. They are often buried on their home reservation and their offspring have theoretical rights to the land.

(3) The *localized lineage* is composed of males who are the agnatic core of the maximal lineage, as well as unmarried lineage females. For reservation-based activities of a traditional nature, the male core of the localized lineage is the most significant suprafamilial aggregate in Mapuche society. As indicated, the localized core today contains branches or sublineages, themselves constituting the most tightly integrated units above the level of the family-household.

(4) These *sublineages* are branches of the maximal lineage formed at different generational levels below that of the founder of the line. Sublineages segment further at each generational level.

(5) One of these levels, which is consonant with the extended-family household, composed of father and married sons, a potential beginning for a new sublineage, may be called the *minimal lineage*.

Lineage-based Kinship Relationships

In getting to know how and why Mapuche interacted with one another, I would generally pose hypothetical problems for them to answer, such as, "Who would you ask to help you prepare your fields" or "Who would you ask to help you harvest your fields if bad weather threatened the crop" or "Why did you ask so-and-so to help you do such-and-such?" Most of the questions of this sort which were asked Alonqueo and others on his and nearby reservations were, frankly, naive, since not much was known about interpersonal relationships in the beginning. Later, after living with Huenchemil and with Luís Nahualpan, I knew pretty much what the answers would be, and my questions served mainly as confirmation of what I had learned in the first few months of fieldwork.

On the reservations a man is thrown into daily relationships with patrilineal kinsmen. He does not go around speaking of his ancestors or even thinking about them, and he does not say to a lineage mate, "Since we are members of the same maximal lineage we ought to do thus-and-so together." Yet the actions and thoughts of all adult males are rooted in the structure of patrilineality and, when questioned about activities and beliefs, the notion of maximal lineage emerges clearly enough for the anthropologist to grasp it.

Alonqueo, my first key informant, would work the fields and perform other chores at the behest of his elder brother—a household arrangement. But he would also work for his (deceased) father's brothers upon request, an obligation which he explained to me as customary law (*admapu*). This is rather different from saying, as we might in our society, that Uncle Joe is a nice fellow and I am going to help him out. It is not even the same as the kind of coercion we are sometimes subjected to in our culture, such as, "As my paternal nephew you ought to respect me and help me when I ask you to." There is really no need to justify requests or demands of this sort among the Mapuche. Everyone learns that this obligation as well as the exercise of certain privileges is *admapu*, and governs his behavior according to such well-defined standards.

On certain occasions, such as helping to repair a bridge over a stream which cuts through the reservation, Alonqueo would work with more distant relatives in *mingaco*. These were "uncles" and "cousins." Alonqueo would work *vuelta mano* with a young paternal uncle and with two cousins, the three relatives being very good friends of his, members of closely connected sublineages on his reservation. He never cooperated in mingaco with affinal relatives, be they mother's kinsmen or those related to him through the marriage of his sister or through marriages of other women of his patrilineage.

Alonqueo loved to visit town, and took every opportunity to get away from agricultural chores or other kinds of work to spend a day away from the reservation. His mother and elder brother chided him for this and considered him lazy because of his lack of interest in household business. He liked to drink his full measure of wine. Still, Alonqueo would not think of going to town alone or of drinking with strangers in town. His visits to town would be determined, therefore, by the availability of kinsmen who would go with him; and not just any kinsmen would do. He had several kinsmen who were "drinking buddies." If they could not go to town, Alonqueo would not go.

If Alonqueo had some cash, which he seldom did, he would invite both of his cousins, who were his age-mates, related to him through great uncles. If he was broke, as he usually was, he would hang around one of his uncles, who was more or less an age-mate, though of a different genealogical generation, waiting for an invitation to accompany him to town, with the understanding that Alonqueo would be his uncle's guest. A person has alternatives within a kinship field by which to achieve his ends. Alonqueo was eager to go to town with me, but was always warning me not to drink with strangers.

Huenchemil is a middle-aged chief who enjoys a status rather different from that of Alonqueo. Huenchemil is a good farmer, a hard worker who sticks to the best of the traditional Mapuche life while considering innovations and improvements coming from contact with Chilean society. A member of the parental generation on his reservation, he enjoys political authority as chief. He is sought out not only by his kinsmen who do him favors, but is also sought out by non-kinsmen on his reservation. His younger "brothers" and his "nephews" actually vie with one another to be of service to him, expecting some kind of patronage in return. Huenchemil manipulates this situation. Alonqueo was not in this position. Alonqueo was the seeker, a reasonably mature man, but too young to be knowledgeable or to have political influence.

One of Huenchemil's nephews worked freely on his land for several years, helping his uncle in many ways. This was explained to me as being a kinship obligation. Huenchemil told me, "It is correct for him to help me," and the young nephew said, "It is right for me to help him." The reasons were phrased in traditional terms of *admapu*. However, there was more to the matter than customary respect. Huenchemil told me that since he had only two sons and a good deal of farmland, he would probably bequeath a few hectares to his young nephew, whose family did not have enough land to parcel out among their sons.

Luís Nahualpan, a zealous Protestant, lived on land that was formerly a reservation, and which had been parcelled out among the several households, upon their request, by government order. Luís worked with no one. He had little faith in his kinsman. Learned in western technology, he produced uniformly good harvests, attributing this good fortune to his conversion to Christianity. His feelings and interpersonal relationships were very different from the vast majority of Mapuche. He refused to speak to his maternal uncle because the man, according to Luís, had professed conversion to Protestantism but continued to participate in the traditional *ñillatun* ceremony. The personal overtones in this relationship are nontraditional.

Luís spoke highly of his ancestors, but did not venerate them spiritually. He spoke well of most Mapuche on his reservation and surrounding reservations, indicating once in a while that so-and-so would be a better man if he allowed himself to be captured by the Lord's Spirit rather than the witch doctor's spirit. His age-mates considered Luís to be *wesa lonko*, which may be translated either as "crazy" or "possessed by an evil spirit." Luís' elders regarded him as a progressive farmer but, it seemed to me, they also looked upon him as somewhat of an outsider. He had spent several years in a missionary school and was away from the reservation when his father deserted his mother, not even returning at that time to comfort the old woman, or to make the usual libations, and so forth. Luís prided himself on his perfect command of Spanish and his modernity. He measured up to most of the traditional obligations he owed his patrilineal kinsmen, considering these a gesture of friendliness, but lacked most of the deep feelings of kinship. This was quite consistent with his conversion to Protestantism.

Dominant and Subordinate Lineages

We have seen that most reservations were mapped and registered in such a way that unrelated households were included in reservation boundaries, even though reservations were supposedly established on a "family" or "lineage" basis. The picture which emerges on the one hand from informants' accounts and on the other from the several thousand reservation titles (and the censuses which these contain) in the registry offices is that on most reservations the man first named or recorded as chief was the acknowledged spokesman of a multihousehold kingroup; and that there were, in addition, one or more households or groups of houses composed of persons who were not kinsmen of the chief. These clusters of aliens (*winka*) were sometimes given asylum on the reservations, and for this reason acknowledged the leadership of the registered chief.

These families which were not related to the chief may be considered "remnant" groups. They were small units of kin left over from once larger and then depleted groups, persons who were at the time leaderless. They also appear to have been relative newcomers to the region, flotsam in the population flux of the time between final military defeat and the establishment of reservation life.

It is clear from some reports that these nonrelated groups acknowledged the leadership of the designated chief of the newly formed reservation, if only because he had lived on that land for a longer period than they. It is equally clear, though, that they sometimes did not acknowledge his leadership, that they in fact did not even fully understand that they were being placed on a reservation under the protection of a chief. The political picture was often clouded because of the failure of Chilean officials and Mapuche leaders to communicate in areas such as this.

The remnant groups have become what can be considered subordinate lineages. Their membership is smaller than that of the lineage of the founding chief, which is the dominant lineage. Their membership has not increased at the same rate as that of the chiefly lineage, largely because most advantages (for example, favorable allotment of land) were enjoyed by members of the chief's lineage. Discontent resulted in members of these subordinate lineages emigrating, leaving the reservation, moving to Argentina or elsewhere in Chile. These lineages are out-voted in the council of elders, when their interest conflicts with that of the present-day chief. They sometimes seem to have initiated (in the past at least) appeals for the disbandment of the reservation community and the allotment by the Chilean government of land in individual title. They are sometimes openly referred to as aliens (*winka*) by the members of the dominant, chiefly lineage, especially in times of strife on the reservation; yet they are incorporated into the reservation community in a number of ways, are delegated ritual responsibility in fertility ceremonies, given administrative roles in reservation-wide labor organization, and so forth. They have even been drawn into a quasikinship relationship with the dominant lineage, since they are considered inappropriate marriage partners in the context of reservation exogamy, as are members of one's own lineage. Their presence on the reservations has made for economic, political, and religious organization of a much more complex, heterogeneous nature than that of prereservation days.

5

Residence Patterns

T HE MAPUCHE believe that it is proper for sons to remain with their father after they marry, bringing their wives to their father's house or compound to live. Historical sources indicate that this is an age-old belief and censuses of a large number of reservations show that there is almost full observance of this patrilocal principal.

Patrilocality

Early Spanish chronicles, as well as books written during the nineteenth century, describe large patrilocal, extended-family households, occupied by a man, his married sons, and grandchildren. These arrangements, although still found today, are not nearly as common as the historical material suggests they may have been in earlier times. In the past, married sons seem frequently to have moved out of the parental household, mainly under the pressure of warfare, to resettle in virgin territory in the Chilean forests or across the Andes in Argentina. It is difficult to judge, therefore, just how tenacious patrilocal organization was in prereservation times.

With respect to residence rules, the Mapuche are no different from many other societies—they make the best approximation possible under given circumstances. It is clear that patrilocal principles are ancient in Mapucheland. What is not so clear are the details of approximation during the prereservation era.

On today's reservations, extended-family households seem to be in the minority, yet extended-family organization persists. This seeming paradox is resolved, however, if we change our perspective from the household to the reservation. Seldom patrilocal by household, today's Mapuche are nearly always patrilocal by reservation. The overwhelming tendency is that a married man continues to live on the reservation of his birth and on his father's land, albeit very often not under his father's roof. If there is still virgin land on the reservation, a man's son may move some distance away from the parental roof, in establishing a household and clearing farmland for its support. For purposes of anthropological classification, how are these domiciliary arrangements to be evaluated?

If married sons set up separate households but continue to work the land under the authority of their father or, after their father's death, continue to work together, it is felt that this is essentially patrilocal organization. If married sons do not continue to work under their father, one may no longer speak of patrilocal residence no matter how close the off-shoot houses may be to one another. It is not only a common roof which defines patrilocality; there must also be a common organizational front.

Alonqueo's case is illustrative of the problems involved in defining a patrilocal organization. His father and father's brother once shared a common roof with Alonqueo's grandfather. Alonqueo was born in his grandfather's house. His father and uncle lived together with their families for several years after the grandfather's death. Alonqueo's uncle subsequently married a second and third time, which was fully in accord with the Mapuche custom of polygyny. However, Alonqueo's mother objected to having to live in a house with so many other women and also objected to the fact that Alonqueo's uncle, who was older than Alonqueo's father, was in control of household organization. She prevailed on Alonqueo's father to set up a separate house.

Alonqueo's father built a house less than 100 meters from his brother's house. He continued to work ancestral land with his brother for many years, long enough so that he also worked jointly with his brother's grown sons. This would be called a patrilocally organized homestead, overlooking of the physical separation of the houses, and emphasizing the human organization.

There came about a political difference between Alonqueo's father and uncle. The two men drew apart, worked together reluctantly for a time and then ceased to cooperate, effecting an allocation of their father's land between them. When I arrived on Alonqueo's reservation members of the two households were not even on speaking terms. In fact they occasionally made charges and counter charges of sorcery. At this juncture, they certainly did not make up a patrilocal social unit, even though their physical positions had not changed. A superficial census of the reservation would not have revealed this condition, which amounted to something more than mere family discord.

The reluctance to break up patrilocal organization in Alonqueo's case shows the force of the patrilocal ideal. But this kind of rupture in patrilocal relationships does not occur often. Huenchemil's case is typical of enduring patrilocal organization over several generations.

There is a registry map for Huenchemil's reservation which was drawn by the original surveyors at the end of the nineteenth century. It shows Huenchemil's grandfather's house on the same site as Huenchemil's present house, barn, and storage shack. The original census also shows that Huenchemil's grandfather's household was a large, extended, patrilocal unit, composed of the grandfather and grandmother, their married sons and grandchildren. Huenchemil now lives with his widowed mother, wife and children. His brothers live nearby, on portions of the land originally held by their grandfather, but in separate houses with their wives and children. The farmland on which Huenchemil and his brothers live has an area of approximately twenty hectares.

In Huenchemil's case, the usual branching-off of households from a former patrilocal extended household has taken place since the grandfather's time. In essence, this is a patrilocal arrangement, even though Huenchemil and his brothers live in separate houses, because the brothers and their families continue to co-operate closely with one another and under the leadership of Huenchemil, who is chief of the reservation. Each brother keeps the harvest from his own fields, but the fields are worked cooperatively, farm equipment is shared, a joint agreement is reached on what crops to sow, when and where to plant them, when and to whom they should be sold, and other similar matters. Ancestral land is kept intact, allotments having been made by Huenchemil's father as his sons married and built houses for their own families.

The most significant break with the patrilocal pattern occurs when a man moves off his natal reservation to live with his wife on her reservation. This kind of situation occurs frequently enough for it to reveal a patterned exception to patrilocality. It may be called uxorilocal residence.

Uxorilocal Residence

Uxor is Latin for wife, and uxorilocal means "in the place of the wife." As applied to the Mapuche, uxorilocal residence means that the husband moves to his wife's reservation to live and raise his family. It is a forced alternative to patrilocal residence and one which, from the man's point of view, involves much readjustment in his way of life. However, it enables the man to remain within Mapuche society; that is, makes it possible for him to live in the country as an Indian. A third alternative is for the man and his wife to abandon reservation life and reside as laborers on a Chilean or Argentine farm or ranch, or to live in a town or city and work as menials or day laborers on the lowest rung of the social ladder. While difficult for the man and his children, uxorilocal residence at least affords them the psychological comfort of life on the reservation.

The most common reason for a man living on his wife's reservation is that farmland has become so scarce and fragmented on his own reservation that he is deprived of sufficient land with which to support a wife and children. Another reason, often given by the Mapuche and indicating something of the difficulties of adjustment of the man in uxorilocal residence, is that such a man must have been evicted from his own reservation, either because he is a thief or murderer or because he is a sorcerer. In checking out these charges in several cases the author found that there was no substance to them. The main reason, therefore, seems to be that scarce land forces men to take up residence on their wife's reservation which they do rather than emigrate to the cities and farms controlled by whites.

A man living uxorilocally, then, does have the advantage of living within the reservation-based culture of the Mapuche and, particularly, of having use-rights to farmland on his wife's reservation. Nevertheless, he chafes about having to live with his in-laws and about not being considered a full-fledged member of the reservation community—in other words, not being able to exercise lineage-based rights.

Huenchulaf (*not* Huenchemil) lived uxorilocally on a reservation near Toltén. He was born in the northern part of Mapucheland on a reservation having scarce farmland. He left home as a young man, served his period of military service, and wandered around Mapucheland for a few years doing odd jobs on Chilean ranches and farms, working sometimes for Mapuche farmers in the harvest season. Finally, he met a young widow on one of these reservations and married her. The widow had returned to her elder brother's house from her husband's reservation after the latter had died. She was barren and, therefore, not a particularly desirable wife.

Huenchulaf married her for two main reasons. He was tired of living the floating, bachelor's life and wanted a wife to take care of his needs; he had found a woman with a claim to land on her natal reservation who was willing to marry a landless man. Huenchulaf told me that life was sometimes difficult for him because his brothers-in-law would remind him that he did not really have any rights on their reservation, that he was allowed to live there only as long as their sister wanted him. He had paid no bride-price for their sister and was, therefore, not legally her husband. He could not produce any grandchildren for them, a fact which they seemed to blame him for rather than their barren sister. Huenchulaf related a series of other kinds of complaints. He put up with such unpleasantness because it only occurred occasionally and because he preferred it to not having a woman of his own or land to work for his own household. Finally, he was able, by the arrangements he had made, to live a fairly traditional life even though deprived of a number of rights he would have enjoyed had he been able to establish his household on the reservation of his birth.

Other men living in uxorilocal residence but having children are in a somewhat different position. They tend to suffer with Huenchulaf the same kinds of slights and, in addition, must see their children deprived of lineage rights. This is more important with respect to their sons than their daughters. The sons have no lineage-based claim to farmland on their mother's reservation. If there is ample land there, the Mapuche say that a young man's mother could exert enough influence on her kinsmen so that he would be provided land on which to build a house and live with his wife and children. Perhaps this occurs on some reservations, although genealogical checking on many reservations I visited failed to reveal such developments.

Nor do such young men have much success in validating their lineage rights if they return to their father's natal reservation to live. It is not difficult for them to move in with paternal kinsmen, if they wish, but on crowded reservations they usually do not obtain farmland to work themselves. On uncrowded reservations they may validate lineage claims to land. Several examples of this came to my attention.

The usual course taken by young men deprived of access to farmland is emigration to Chilean farms and cities or career service in the army or national police force—or uxorilocal residence.

6

The Status of Women

COMPARED TO MEN, women have a generally inferior position in Mapuche society. Yet all females do not have the same status, and within each particular role, there is another hierarchy. The status of married women, for instance, differs from unmarried women; that of mothers from childless women. Wives in a polygynous household are ranked and treated differently. Specialists, such as shamans and sorcerers, have positions very different from ordinary women. Age differences also affect female status.

Unmarried Women

A girl grows to womanhood on her father's reservation. In terms of lineage organization, and kinship and marriage in general, her most important relatives are men and women of her own lineage. With respect to lineage organization, her mother is an outsider and her mother's lineal kinsmen are both physically and socially somewhat remote from everyday life. They are relatives of a completely different kind from those of her own lineage.

Mapuche women often marry before they are twenty years old, and until that time, are not considered fully adult. Household life, for a girl, is highly regulated. They perform domestic and farm chores under the supervision of their mother and father who control all their activities. They make no decisions of their own. In fact, they must ask permission to leave the house, even if they merely intend to visit a neighbor's house. They tend to be saddled with the least attractive household duties and the ones requiring the least skill. They are, in short, helpers.

Only in Alonqueo's house did I have the opportunity to observe the daily behavior of two unmarried girls and to talk to them about their plans for the future, their feelings about present conditions, and so forth. Cross-checking in other households indicated that these observations are a fairly typical form of family life.

Manuela was eleven years old and eight years younger than Juanita. Their mother, also called Manuela, was just under sixty years of age. The eleven-year old spoke poor Spanish, while Juanita spoke quite good Spanish. The mother spoke no Spanish at all. The three of them tutored me in Araucanian during my first few months in Mapucheland.

Manuela was the darling of her mother, the last and unexpected child; but Juanita was her mother's main helper and, because of the old woman's age, actually managed a good deal of the cooking, the cleaning, and the barnyard chores. Juana and her younger sister were very affectionate to one another, held hands while seated near the open fire, deloused one another, confided in each other, and had secrets from their mother and brothers (which they delighted in telling me), and were generally most compatible. Nonetheless, Juanita dominated Manuela.

Since there were no young boys in the family, Manuela performed most of the chores ordinarily done by males, such as bringing the cattle into the corral after they had ranged the fallowed fields and grasslands, collecting firewood, feeding the pigs, running errands, and so on. Juanita did not usually do any of these things and, when told to do any of them because Manuela was busy at something else, performed them grudgingly. She complained to me once in a while that it was alright for Manuela to do boy's chores but that she was a young woman ready for marriage and found the work demeaning. When she was angry with her mother or elder brothers, for having made her do something which she thought was beneath her (that is, not befitting her status as a nubile woman), she tended to become severe with Manuela and would even make a point of not sitting next to her or her mother at the fire when we were eating or telling stories at night.

Juanita had no sweetheart and had had no sexual experience. Her mother would tease her about this, while Manuela listened wide-eyed and somewhat amused. It is doubtful that the author's presence embarrassed them when sexual matters were discussed or when jokes about sex were made. In fact, I found that Mapuche women spoke rather freely about sex to me and to Mapuche men, and would even repeat indelicate comments they had made so that they could be recorded phonetically. Both men and women would then help me with the Spanish translation of the Araucanian text.

Juanita was a pretty girl and, therefore, ran little risk of becoming a spinster, even though she had passed the age when most Mapuche girls have lovers. Manuela was young enough to blush when her family joked with her about marrying either me or one of the boys she knew from school, especially if the joke had anything to do with becoming a second wife in a polygynous household and moving far away. Mapuche women move away to live on their husband's reservation but, in the author's presence, "far away" had the added meaning of going somewhere north of Chile—to the United States.

There are few spinsters in Mapucheland. A definition of spinsterhood is difficult to make, and the main reason for discussing spinsters is to show that this status is an extreme alternative for a Mapuche woman. Without having convincing numerical evidence of this, I nevertheless feel that most if not all Mapuche spinsters are homosexual or have suffered a tremendous psychological blow—the death of a lover, for instance—which inhibits interest in a normal married life.

(My information on female homesexuality is confined almost entirely to shamans and their novices.)

Unlike males of their lineage, women are usually not lifelong members of their local descent group, and move away from their natal reservation upon marriage. Their views are not taken into consideration by lineage elders when decisions are made about the allocation of house sites and farmland. They have no voice in reservation politics either, and do not take an adult part in funeral or agricultural fertility ceremonies. They help mother, brother, and father with household chores and are entirely household oriented in daily affairs. Their importance is peripheral to that of the male core of the localized lineage to which they belong. However, they do participate in many other reservation-based activities, under the direction of elder females and males.

Married Women

Upon marriage, a woman leaves the reservation of her birth to live out her years on her husband's reservation among his lineage mates and their wives. The Mapuche, men and women alike, are unanimous in their opinion that newly married women are usually very uncomfortable in their in-laws' house or patrilocal compound. It is also generally agreed, however, that, as years go by, married women make a comfortable adjustment to life on their husband's reservation. Central to this adjustment, more often than not, is the death of the mother-in-law.

Brides are hen-pecked by their mother-in-law and, sometimes, by the older unmarried sisters of their husband. The death of the mother-in-law, or her senility and relinquishment of domestic authority, and the marriage and moving-off of the sisters-in-law, leave the field open to the inmarried woman. As she takes over the main domestic duties of her father-in-law's household or compound, her position on her husband's reservation is enhanced. And this is not the only method of improving her status.

Motherhood enhances a woman's prestige on her husband's reservation. The Mapuche want many children and place a great value on women who produce many children who survive infancy. As we shall see, this is part of the Mapuche system of religious values, an integral part of which is ancestor propitiation. Proper appeasement of ancestors depends on numerous descendants, especially males.

Women are not treated with especial tenderness when they become pregnant, but they are accorded special social recognition. They are on the threshold of full membership among their husband's family and lineage.

The birth of a child is an arduous event among the Mapuche, one surrounded by stylized behavior, prayer, and magical acts. While the birth of a daughter is welcomed, that of a son is the occasion for great celebration. But a woman's status as mother depends less on the number of sons she has produced than on the fact that she is fertile. She suffers through childbirth as much with a daughter as a son. This event is her admission ticket to adult female status on her husband's reservation, a position not enjoyed by her husband's lineage sisters!

A woman's care of her husband's children attracts the attention of all the members of her husband's lineage, since she is, in a manner of speaking, the guardian of offspring of the lineage. She has certain well-defined rights on her husband's reservation, a concommitant of traditional obligations. She must participate in institutional activities on her husband's reservation, in the course of which she becomes fully integrated into the reservation community.

Some women, of course, fail to produce children, or give birth to children who die in infancy. Barrenness, in this amplified sense, suggests moral failure or evilness to most Mapuche. They judge the woman herself to be evil or feel that she has somehow become contaminated by forces of evil, which is much the same thing. Barrenness is ground for divorce.

Barren women are not always divorced, however, especially if they are physically attractive and are good workers. But a man with a barren wife (a woman who has not conceived within the first few years of marriage), often thinks about taking an additional wife. There is nothing in my field material, though, which suggests polygynous households develop as a solution to the barrenness of the primary wife. Nor is there anything in the literature about the Mapuche suggesting this; but the Mapuche say that most polygnists are either concupiscent or have a barren wife. Here we are enmeshed in the tangle between observation of polygynous households (statistical) and statements of how things should be (ideal), and is merely suggested as a research problem to student readers, without making the effort to solve it in this case study.

Polygny exists as a male ideal, however, and regardless of barrenness of a man's first wife, polygynous houses continue to form in Mapucheland. Sexual prowess is involved in this ideal, but even more important is the religious justification for polygyny: the more offspring a man has, the more likely his spirit will be propitiated. Polygyny and the eternal well-being of the soul evidence a high correlation in Mapucheland.

Polygynous wives are ranked in a rough order. Assuming that wives are more or less equally competent to perform their duties, the first wife, and the eldest, is the principal wife. She manages the household or compound and she is the main helpmate of the husband. The second or third wife is almost always younger and more physically attractive than the first wife. The husband's sexual attentions are usually diverted from the primary wife when he takes an additional woman. However, brideprice is seldom paid for the additional wives or, if paid, is much less and involves much less ostentation than with the initial marriage. This indicates that the social status of the primary wife is higher than that of secondary wife, a conclusion which is forced by observing the interaction among polygynous wives. The primary wife rules the roost.

As to women who have some kind of special status, aside from those who have reputations for being the best potters, and weavers, we have only to consider shamans and sorcerers. The Mapuche feel that shamans and sorcerers are social deviants. Nevertheless, their services are acknowledged as necessary to the preservation of Mapuche society, and an analysis of their status will be taken up in later chapters.

7

Sex and Courtship

IN THE PROCESS of obtaining information about the kinship system (in discussing the arrangement of kin terms and their relation to genealogies) it was possible to elicit a certain amount of information about sex, love, and courtship which, in turn, provide clues for further inquiry. Since I found it rather difficult to persuade men and boys to talk about love and sex in formal interviews I had to compile innumerable piecemeal remarks in order to form a general picture of their views. Working with adult women informants, however, it was possible to ask questions systematically. I would work alone when interviewing Spanish-speaking women and use an interpreter, preferably a female, when working with monolingual women. It was very difficult, however, to catch chance remarks made by women, since I did not understand Araucanian well enough and they were usually unable to translate into Spanish, as men did.

Courtship, characterized by a love affair, is the customary prelude to marriage, and involves notions of beauty, honor, virtue, and other qualities which are easily enough understood by the visitor to Mapucheland. Romantic notions are usually tempered by considerations of a practical nature, such as the industriousness, ability, and compatibility of the intended spouse. This is the Mapuche consensus.

However, very few Chileans would agree with the above statement and, indeed, it took a few months in Mapucheland before I could see the validity of the consensus. What is clear is that Chilean views of Mapuche sex life and marriage customs are colored not so much by observation as by unsubstantiated tales based on what they have heard or read about the Mapuche: stories of widespread incest, extramarital affairs, and so on. These stories are made to dovetail with known customs, such as polygyny, first-cousin marriage, and others antithetical to Catholic belief.

Before discussing love and sex in the framework of courtship, let us look at some of the points cited by Chileans as evidence that the Mapuche are concupiscent savages. Then let us see how the Mapuche define moral and immoral sexual relationships, and place the Chilean view in perspective.

Illicit Sexual Relations: Chilean Views

Early ethnographic reports mention that the Mapuche committed all degrees of incest, even between mother and son. As I have indicated in an earlier study such statements are very dubious and seem not to square with the verifiable facts of Mapuche life. Yet one of these dubious bits of information deserves mention: the custom of a son inheriting his father's wives with whom he then has sexual relations. This is known as filial inheritance of wives.

Filial inheritance of wives occurs in a number of patrilineal societies, and it is a custom known to the Mapuche. Among the Mapuche of the past, there is some indication that a man had sexual relations with one or more of his younger widowed stepmothers, but never with his own mother. There is no evidence to show that this was ever a widespread practice and indeed there is much evidence to the contrary. Furthermore, it is a custom which is consistent with Mapuche ideas about lineage rights that have been established over women through the payment of brideprice, and is not a breach of traditional morality. What seems to have happened is that the occasional observance of this custom in the past has been blown out of proportion by Chileans, who maintain that it continues to occur among the Mapuche.

Polygyny itself is repugnant to Chileans. Although it has long been a Mapuche custom, it seems to be diminishing today, partly for reasons of economic hardship and partly because of changes in Mapuche values. Chileans say that the polygynist is concupiscent and feels no tenderness towards his multiple wives; that the women who live under such an arrangement are little better than animals. Mapuche men and women alike deny these charges.

The frequency of rape among the Mapuche is exaggerated too by the Chileans. In any case, rape occurs among Chileans and, in that sense, cannot be considered an especially primitive practice.

Extramarital affairs occur frequently among the Mapuche; frequently among Chileans. Each side tends to exaggerate the other's propensities.

The most heinous commission of incest, according to the Chilean view, is that already mentioned and dismissed: filial access to father's widows. There are, however, ongoing Mapuche customs which constitute incest from the Catholic Chilean point of view. These are first-, second-, and third-cousin marriages for which the Mapuche do not receive special permission from the Church. Since marriages of this sort are widespread, the Chileans are, from their way of looking at the custom, correct in stating that incest is widespread. The fact that these marriages are sometimes arranged by the parents of the cousins adds to the revulsion felt by Chileans. The Chilean observation is only genealogically correct, however, and it indicates the great cultural gulf between Chilean and Mapuche societies.

Illicit Sexual Relations: Mapuche Views

When asked directly about filial inheritance of wives, the Mapuche, according to their interpretation of the question, are sometimes at a loss to confirm or deny the existence of the custom. What those who say that filial inheritance of wives does *not* take place really mean is that a son does not have sexual access to his mother and step-mothers. Those who deny this custom altogether, and add that it is repugnant to them, I suspect of dissembling before the outsider. The reason for the doubt is because of the other kind of answer which is often given. Many Mapuche say that filial inheritance does occur, citing examples, indicating that a son inherits the *obligation* to support his father's widows and say that it is the same thing as the responsibility a son owes his widowed mother. Although I do not pretend to have explored all the possibilities, I am willing to dismiss the sexual and therefore incestuous implications of the Chilean view.

Polygyny is of course not incestuous nor is it illicit according to the Mapuche. A polygynist, especially a rather old man, is sometimes referred to (in front of the anthropologist, at least) as lascivious, but men do not berate him for taking additional wives. Rather, younger men tend to say that the custom is dying out and that only the elders seriously consider becoming polygynists.

As to rape, the Mapuche punish offenders as least as severely as Chileans. When identified and caught a rapist is beaten by the closest male relatives of the woman and, in their anger, sometimes even kill him.

Of greater sociological importance are Mapuche ideas about incest and lineage exogamy which relate to a marriage system unknown to unlettered Chileans. The marriage system has been briefly mentioned in Chapter 6 and will be described in other respects in Chapters 8 and 9. In this chapter we will consider sexual relations outside the context of marriage, albeit somewhat arbitrarily.

A man may have sexual intercourse with any woman he may marry, pre- and extra-marital relationships being restricted primarily by considerations of incest rather than chastity, fidelity, and so forth. Under these rules a man may have an affair with any unmarried woman of his mother's patrilineal descent group or with a woman from any other patrilineage related to his own through the marriage of any of his lineage brothers (agnates). All of these women are called by the same kinship term, *ñuke*, which may be translated as marriageable woman, and is the word used for wife and sweetheart. All of these women are on one "side" of the family. In addition, a man may have sexual intercourse with any other woman in Mapuche society who is not related to him. This leaves two large categories of woman with whom a man is forbidden sexual access: lineage sisters and descendants of lineage sisters (who are on the other "side" of the family). It is easy to tell who these persons are by the kinship terms applied to them.

Within this larger context, incestuous relations occasionally occur, as well as relations which, while not actually incestuous, may well lead to social discord and animosities between families.

An incestuous union never leads to marriage. The community would never give their approval. Once the relationship comes to the community's attention, the offending pair is ordered to break off their relationship. If they are young enough to be unaware of their crime, they may simply be admonished for it. If they are adults, they are often beaten, sometimes evicted from the reservation. On rare occasions they throw tradition to the winds and abandon reservation life of their own accord.

While I was living with Alonqueo an incestuous affair on a nearby reservation came to my attention. If the air was not actually buzzing with gossip about this affair, it was discussed enough so that I was able to grasp the seriousness of it even with a very imperfect understanding of the language and the rules which had been broken. A young man and his "cousin" (classificatory sibling—that is, "sister") from another sublineage of his patrilineal descent group were having a sexual relationship. Although it was not common knowledge, certain relatives either knew about the affair or suspected it. It was finally brought to the attention of the young man's older brother, after which it ceased. Because the man and the girl were young, they were merely admonished by receiving a detailed account of the rules of proper marriage on one hand and what constitutes incest on the other. This was really my first (and there were but few others) example of incest and, luckily for me, it was discussed with great thoroughness in my presence, on which occasions I was permitted to ask for clarification, present hypothetical examples of incest, compare Mapuche and American views of incest, and so forth. (Compare this with example cited in Faron 1961:165–166.)

A more serious and unfortunate example is that of Antemil, who lived on a reservation near Toltén. Antemil went to live with his father's sister, a childless widow, on the reservation to which she had moved upon marriage. This was at his aunt's request. She asked Antemil's father to send one of his sons to help support her. Since there was a shortage of land on Antemil's reservation, his father was willing for him to move away and even entertained his marriage to a young woman from that general vicinity, which might have led to uxorilocal residence. After several years had passed without Antemil indicating a desire to marry, his kinsmen began to feel that "something must be wrong." Antemil returned to live in his father's house and announced that his aunt was pregnant and that people were blaming it on him. He and his aunt denied the implied incestuous relationship. Investigating the matter, Antemil's father became convinced that they had committed incest and Antemil left his father's house in disgrace. The aunt failed to abort the fetus and gave birth to a son. The infant, while still very young, fell into the open fire and was badly burned on the legs. Antemil's father took care of the child after his mother abandoned him and, presumably, went to live in Santiago.

The child "had no place," no lineage membership. At the time of my stay near Toltén, the child was partially crippled, although several years had passed since the accident. His mother's brother, who was looking after him, had built him a special stroller onto which he could hold while walking. He was referred to as his mother's brother's "son," in order to lessen and perhaps eventually eradicate the stigma of his birth. Nevertheless, several lives were ruined because of incest, not to mention the larger number of persons who feared some sort of supernatural reprisal because of their kinship to the incestuous pair.

Relationships which may lead to social discord but which are not in any sense incestuous are those in which one person, almost always the man, has no intention of marrying the other. The Mapuche feel that sexual experimentation is natural and even desirous, but they also try to keep it under control. They do this by urging their children to settle down to married life after a few year's sexual freedom or by curtailing sexual freedom. If a romance seems not to be leading to a formal courtship and to eventual marriage, the parents of the girl restrict her to the house and discourage the young man from seeing her. If the man is already married, and seems to have no intention of seeking an additional wife (something which may be learned by sounding out his wife or relatives), the relationship may be broken up rather easily. Word may be passed to his wife that he is sexually involved with a younger woman and that both families are being put to shame. This could cause sufficient domestic strain to put an end to the affair. Still, if the man is considered desirable by the girl's parents, the opposite may occur. They may bring pressure to bear on the man, his wife, and his closest kinsmen to negotiate marriage. They may even encourage their daughter to become pregnant, strengthening her chances. What may actually result from troublesome sexual affairs is highly situational, depending on the motives and the consequences involved.

Courtship

Although courtship involves trysts and lovers' secrets it is not itself a secret affair. It is, for example, distinguishable from all the clandestine sexual affairs mentioned above. Courtship is open and above-board; it has social approval; it is known to the community and discussed widely. It should lead to a traditional marriage which is celebrated by the community. Its public acknowledgement is a commitment that marriage will take place in due course.

The chances are overwhelming that the young couple have known one another since childhood, that their parents are kinsmen related through a number of former marriages, that they have been visitors in each other's houses and, nowadays, that they have attended the reservation school together. As children it is likely that they were playmates, teased one another, fought against one another or together against others. Whatever the details of their childhood relationships may be, one thing is certain—they were close. Mapuche tend not to court or marry strangers, only kinsmen. These kinsmen live on nearby reservations and are persons with whom they meet year after year at funerals, agricultural fertility ceremonies, harvest festivities, soccer games and, more recently, nontraditional fiestas which celebrate Chilean Independence and other national events.

Alonqueo told me that he used to chase the little girls home from school, playing with them, taunting them, and so forth, and that for years he thought of them equally. When he was twelve years old or so, his father spoke to him of manhood and, among many other matters associated with becoming a man, told him something of the rules of marriage. Alonqueo told the story with ample use of kinship terms and paraphrased his father's lecture by providing brief, idealized versions of how certain relatives should be treated. Out of this came the insistence that the only girl a decent boy should have anything to do with is *ñuke*, and that besides beauty one should look to her industriousness and truthfulness as major personal qualities.

Alonqueo's version is typical of what younger males have to tell the anthropologist. Older men talk more about what they have told their sons. Young girls tell the anthropologist very little, except that they are going to marry their *ñillan*, provided they are able to find one who is not worthless. Older women's statements complement those of the males, although they provide more information about the virtues of their daughters, what proper marriage means to a girl, and so forth.

Long hours were spent talking with Alonqueo while both of us worked in the fields or while simply sitting in the house or under a tree. I feel I knew Alonqueo better than any of my informants and I had the opportunity to watch his courtship develop into marriage. It is fitting, therefore, to conclude with his story.

Alonqueo may be described as happy-go-lucky, even a bit shiftless, if one were to accept his mother's judgment. He was the second son, which, in his case, meant that his elder brother would inherit the family house and live there with his wife and children. The elder brother had not yet married and seemed to be in no hurry to do so. He had control of all the family's resources and was a good looking, strapping fellow who enjoyed himself with several girls on different reservations. In a sense, however, he was standing in Alonqueo's way.

Alonqueo, because of his subordinate position in the household and because his brother had not yet married and because family land was scarce, was reluctant to marry his sweetheart. Alonqueo's father had died some years before, leaving the land and house in trust with his wife but under the effective supervision of his elder son. No separate provision had been made for Alonqueo to receive a parcel of the family land for his own use when he married. It was understood that he would live with his brother and mother and sisters in the old house. When Alonqueo became serious about marriage, however, he discussed with the family the possibility of setting up a separate household and taking part of the fields for his particular use. The mother and elder brother were reluctant to split the holdings, but were vague about their decision (perhaps so as not to talk Alonqueo out of marriage).

Alonqueo was deeply in love, even if reluctant to marry, and spent every spare moment with his sweetheart, who lived a little over a mile away on an adjacent reservation. Her mother almost never failed to mention something about marriage in Alonqueo's presence and, when I visited alone, even mentioned the matter to me. Alonqueo's sister, a friend of his sweetheart, also urged him to marry, but in the typical teasing manner of sisters. His mother spoke to him about settling down and no longer wasting so much time in his sweetheart's house and, as she put it, bothering his "uncle" (*weku:* any male of the mother's lineage from the point of view of Alonqueo).

There were few people on either reservation who did not know something of the courtship and the fact that it had been prolonged for reasons other than faintheartedness. One of Alonqueo's paternal uncles offered him lodging in his house until Alonqueo could arrange to acquire part of his father's land for himself, but Alonqueo declined the offer. *Weku* also offered to give his daughter a good piece of land which Alonqueo could farm for himself. Alonqueo also turned down this offer, because of the difficultis of uxorilocal residnece (even in cases where the reservations are nearby) and because Alonqueo feared the domination of his potential father-in-law.

Alonqueo had some grand schemes. He would join the army and make his fortune. He would go to Argentina for a few years and come back to his bride with riches. He would attend high school in Temuco and learn a trade to enable him to live in town. However, tuberculosis prevented him from serving his year of military service and, in reality, he had no great desire to live in Argentina, although he often spoke of making a visit. In addition, he could not have entered high school because of his lack of educational background and probably knew that Mapuche did not often succeed in towns as tradesmen.

Finally his sweetheart became pregnant. He eloped with her one night and, in the traditional manner, took her to his father's (mother's) house, after which her parents were notified. They agreed to the forthcoming marriage. The month before I left Chile they were married according to Mapuche custom and moved into Alonqueo's parental house to live for an indefinite period.

8

Marriage

THE ACCOUNT of Alonqueo's courtship and marriage, while exemplifying such variables as patrilocal residence patterns, the effects of scarce land on making decisions about marriage, how pregnancy may serve to step up the marriage plans, the Mapuche reluctance to reside uxorilocally (even if it may appear to be to one's economic advantage), and other things, does leave out many details of Mapuche marriage customs. Let us now look at some of the general outlines of the Mapuche marriage system, how marriages are arranged, and whom one can and cannot marry.

Matrilateral Marriage

In discussing certain incestuous relationships, a description of the path along which a young man meanders, from courtship to marriage, was neglected. This path, while usually bounded by clusters of young women related to him through a former marriage that was contracted by any of the males of his lineage, always leads him outside the boundaries of his reservation community in his search for a spouse.

The path is not open to marrying a woman related to him through the marriage of any of his lineage sisters, however. He may not marry a woman of his own lineage either. Custom seems to dictate that he should not marry any woman born on his reservation, whether a relative or not.

A man may marry an unrelated woman from another reservation, but this is not easy to accomplish and such women are not sought after. Mapuche marry relatives almost without exception. What we have in Mapucheland, therefore, are reservation-based lineages whose members intermarry a number of times on any generation and have so married for a number of generations.

These lineages, however, do not intermarry in a haphazard fashion. Rather, men from lineage x marry women from lineage y but give their daughters in marriage to men of lineage z, never to men from lineage y, which would constitute incest. This is merely another way of stating what was discussed in the last chapter: a man can marry a woman connected to him on his mother's side of the family but is forbidden to marry a woman connected to him through the marriage of his lineage sister. In genealogical terms, this may be stated as follows: a man can marry a woman in the category of "mother's brother's daughter" but is forbidden to marry a woman in the category of "father's sister's daughter."

In terms of geneological categories, the ideal form of marriage in the Mapuche scheme is "mother's brother's daughter" marriage. The only departure from this ideal occurs when a man marries a totally unrelated woman. Once such a breach of the ideal occurs, however, the lineage of this woman becomes "related" to that of her husband, as a genealogically defined "mother's brother's daughter's" lineage.

The Mapuche pay much less attention to genealogical ramifications than the anthropologist does, and it is misleading to phrase their notions of a perfect marriage in genealogical terms. Rather, the Mapuche have to know only one thing in order to contract proper marriage: the girl he calls ñuke is the ideal marriage partner.

Readers who have not spent time thinking about marriage systems in other societies might well have found this discussion hard to follow. The following example should make the opening statement intelligible.

Marriage Negotiations

Marriage is entered into with the approval of the families of the bride and groom. In the overwhelming number of cases these families are already related through marriage, the young man's father having married a woman of the lineage to which the young girl belongs, a young man's mother and sweetheart belonging to the same lineage. Regardless of the exact genealogical relationship, the girl's father is weku to the young man.

All of the principals have known one another for years. It is also likely that for at least a year or so they have been thinking about the possibility of the marriage in question, and that some vague commitments about the marriage have been made by both parties. In the absence of family approval, marriage could not take place in the traditional manner, for there would be no brideprice[1] paid, no dowry provided, no house-building arrangements made, and, most importantly, no allotment of family farmland to the newly married couple.

Nontraditional marriages do occur, but with the usual result that the married pair either moves off the reservation, forsaking its Mapuche heritage, or else resides uxorilocally. A consideration of the rare Mapuche-Chilean marriages will not be made here.

---

[1] Items of wealth paid by groom and/or his relatives to bride's relatives to establish rights over her by the groom and his lineage.

According to written and oral descriptions of marriage around the turn of the century and before, marriage negotiations and ceremonies were very much as they are today. The most important changes are understandable as a consequence of adjustments made to reservation life. As in the past, today's marriages may be considered as having three main features: elopement, negotiation, formal ceremony. As in Alonqueo's case, sometimes a good deal of the negotiation is hammered out before elopement, elopement being triggered by pregnancy and serving to bring negotiations to their final stage.

Elopement takes the form of what anthropologists sometimes call "dramatized bride capture," and consists of the young man stealing his intended bride from her family precincts. Sometimes this is done secretly and quietly, as Alonqueo did it; sometimes the bride's family is alerted and put up a mock battle to prevent the abduction of the girl. Since the marriage has been in the offing, usually for some time, the parents of the bride (and groom) are not actually surprised, although they are seldom aware of the exact day and hour. The capture and the resistance are staged. All marriages do not begin this way. Those following long and careful planning of brideprice and dowry may well occur without elopement. Elopement and dramatized capture serve to speed things up, to bring matters to a head.

Wedding arrangements (either after elopement or in its absence) are discussed in advance of the marriage ceremony. The groom-to-be has talked over his forthcoming marriage plans with his father and mother, his elder brothers, his paternal uncles, their wives, and even the chief of the reservation. This has been done both formally and informally. He has often obtained commitments from paternal kinsmen to make at least token contributions of brideprice, trying to make the moveable wealth transferred to the father of the bride as ostentatious as possible, including the finest cattle, horses, sheep, and so forth. He has exacted some commitment from his father and/or grandfather to allot him a sufficient piece of the household's farmland on which he may erect a new house (Alonqueo's case indicating the kinds of difficulties which may be faced). Discussions of a roughly similar sort have been going on in the bride's household and among her patrilineal kinsmen. These involve planning an ostentatious dowry and determining just how much brideprice to demand as suitable to her status.

The principal members of the two families meet and try to reach a preliminary agreement with respect to brideprice and dowry and discuss the main features of the wedding ceremony itself. When these sets of parents are actually affines through previous marriages between their respective lineages, such negotiations are relatively easy to work out; they are reached, at least roughly, in an atmosphere of confidence which would not exist if the groups were not already in the relation of wife-giver and wife-receiver. Other close kinsmen are frequently involved in these discussions which are cloaked in formality. (Alonqueo's elder brother and his paternal uncle substituted for his deceased father.) There is haggling, but no anger or suspicion. Agreement is always reached, provided the parties are serious to begin with. The date for the wedding is set.

The wedding takes place near the house of the bride to which the groom and members of his household and lineage proceed with much dignity, bringing many gifts of food. At Alonqueo's wedding, I was already at the bride's house drinking wine with her father and brothers, watching the women prepare their share of the marriage feast. The solemnity of Alonqueo's party was in such contrast to their behavior on other occasions that I had to struggle not to smile. Even the bride's mother made a little joke about how stiff they all looked. Nevertheless, this is in strict accordance with Mapuche ideas of the social superiority of the wife-giving group and is no laughing matter.

There is further discussion of brideprice and dowry, mainly so that those present for the first time may be impressed with its amount and quality. At this time, again, the groom's father speaks of the land he has given to his son, this being the principal item in brideprice, without which traditional marriage could not take place. A separate parcel of land does not actually have to be ceded to the newly-weds, although this is the best arrangement, but it has to be made clear that a provision of rights to land is made for the bride, and that she have the protection of her husband's lineage mates in order to enjoy these rights.

After these introductory remarks, the groom with several mounted friends, gallops into the midst of the crowd, driving before him a steer (or horse or several sheep) which is presented to the father of the bride as a special gift, not as part of the brideprice. Alonqueo was an excellent horseman and, in his finest *huaso* clothing, cut a magnificent figure as he drove the gift-horse at a gallop to within a few yards of his father-in-law. He had been practicing this entrance with his friends for some time, back on his own reservation, and the horses were glistening with sweat and had traces of foam at the mouth. The dust they kicked up, the animal smells, and the sweaty virility of the groom made for a very impressive entrance. Alonqueo told and retold the story every time he got drunk thereafter.

The gift-animal and others are slaughtered and prepared for the wedding feast. The ceremony lasts well into the night at the bride's father's house. The bride, the groom, his family and kinsmen, return to the groom's house where they too continue to celebrate by singing, dancing, drinking, and eating until the small hours. Three or four days later, the bride, groom, and his mother and father visit the house of the bride's parents bringing with them a slaughtered sheep as a special and final gift, a token of lasting good will and respect. Life then returns to a more normal pattern.

There is a change in the domestic activities in the houses of both bride and groom after a marriage occurs. The bride moves to her husband's reservation and often takes up temporary residence in her father-in-law's house. This change in household composition complicates interpersonal relations across the board. My wife and I (we could have been Alonqueo's brother and sister-in-law) lost our corner of the house and had to move closer to the mother and sisters.

The lot of the bride is at best awkward, usually strained, and sometimes almost unbearable. If there is enough land on the reservation, particularly under the control of the groom's family or sublineage, then the bride and groom build a separate house for themselves apart from that of the groom's father. If not, they either put up a small house in the groom's father's compound or reside under his roof.

Secondary Marriage, Separation, Divorce

There remains only to consider briefly secondary marriage, separation, "divorce," and unmarried adults. Secondary marriages include the taking of an additional wife while the first wife lives, which constitutes a polygynous arrangement, or remarrying after the first wife dies or permanently separates herself from her husband. Almost every reservation has one or more polygynous households or compounds. Nevertheless, quantitative data over a fifty year period seem to indicate that polygyny is declining among the Mapuche. Most secondary marriages, therefore, involve remarriage after the death of the spouse and are themselves monogamous arrangements.

On Huenchemil's reservation, an excellent opportunity was afforded to observe, not only a polygynous household in its daily operation, but an additional marriage of the polygnist. Also, there was a forestalled (subsequent) marriage, when the old man thought of marrying for the second time during our stay. No methodological technique of research could have improved on just-plain-luck in this instance.

The polygnist's name was Pablo and he was paternal great-uncle of the chief, Huenchemil. Altogether Pablo had had five wives, but never more than three at one time. He was living with three wives when I came to know him. Two of the wives lived in the large house and the latest wife lived in a small hut nearby. She is the one referred to in Chapter 9, in the discussion of troublesome affairs.

Pablo paid a good brideprice for this girl but also received a good dowry. Pablo had plenty of land and a large number of cattle and horses besides many sheep, pigs, and so forth. He was a fairly well-to-do Mapuche farmer, one of the reasons he could spend so much time in Toltén drinking and visiting prostitutes.

Pablo's two wives complained to him and to neighbors about his conduct with the third and, as a result, put a temporary halt to his attentions to her after they banded together to prevent his fourth marriage to another young girl. He would often tell the new wife to leave the big house and go to her shack. Then he would leave me with his other wives while he went to see her. They would call him "animal" and *wekufe* (evil spirit), both in his absence and in his presence, and he would respond by ignoring them, when sober, or clouting them, when drunk.

When Pablo told me of his intention to marry again, I made the usual comment about his virility but wondered about how this would affect an already difficult household situation. He had been thinking about this, too, but in his own way. He was mainly concerned about how his youngest wife might feel and told me that he planned to tell her that he was going to marry the fourth wife to gain another heir and to provide the two hags with a helper around the house. Unfortunately, the wives did not accept this story.

Needless to say, Mapuche men have much greater freedom in arranging secondary marriages than women. Widows, if they wish to remarry and to retain rights over land acquired with their first marriage, must marry a lineage mate of their dead husband and remain on their husband's reservation. A woman with a number of small children usually finds it difficult to remarry, and must often content herself with living on her deceased husband's land and receiving protection from her affinal kinsmen. Under these circumstances, she may well take one of them or someone else as an occasional lover.

Couples who are incompatible do separate, for greater or shorter periods of time. Strictly speaking, there is no divorce procedure among the Mapuche, no special ceremony which constitutes a divorce action (such as returning the brideprice). Prolonged separation, however, when there is clearly no intention to reunite, may be said to constitute permanent separation or "divorce." After this, either spouse may take up residence with another partner. There is no marriage ceremony in these cases, again indicating that the Mapuche lack a concept of divorce.

Children of such informal, secondary unions, while generally recognized as belonging to their biological father's lineage, are in an unenviable position. They are not so much stigmatized by the free union of their parents (although this works against them), as they are jeopardized in the exercise of their lineage-based rights, since they have not been legitimatized by the payment of brideprice. Something of the same may be said about the younger children who return with their mother to her natal reservation, in cases of permanent separation. While they are legitimate successors and heirs to their father's position and wealth, because of their absence during childhood, their father has usually committed himself to one or more of the older sons who remained with him at the time of the family separation. Scarce land is an important factor in this regard. There are a number of variables in this matter, but an acceptable generalization would be that one must remain with his father's group in order to validate his lineage-based rights to land, and so on. Separation works to the disadvantage of those off-spring who leave with their mother. They have no lineage-based rights on their mother's reservation.

Finally, there is the matter of bachelors and spinsters. There are few unmarried adults in Mapucheland. Marriage is a Mapuche goal and is fulfilled almost completely. Men and women want children for a number of reasons, not the least of which is the joy they bring and the comfort they lend in old age; and very important is the desire for offspring to propitiate one's spirit after death. Unmarried persons usually do not remain on the reservations, but drift to the cities. Women become servants, or unskilled factory workers, or prostitutes. Men join the ranks of the army and national police force, or seek employment as unskilled manual laborers in the cities, on farms, or on ranches of Chile and Argentina.

9

Domestic Life

Hᴏᴡ ᴅᴏᴇs ᴛʜᴇ ᴀɴᴛʜʀᴏᴘᴏʟᴏɢɪsᴛ make judgments about domestic life after spending only one year living among the Mapuche and spending most of that year living in only three households? In general, it is accomplished by observing what goes on in the three households, by noting the similarities and the differences, and by comparing these to other families in the course of numerous visits.

Family Types

The elementary-family household has emerged from its traditionally larger, extended-family framework to become the basic unit in those agricultural activities which are geared to a regional Chilean market. One might expect that domestic life has undergone marked change since the beginning of the reservation period, largely because of its increasingly autonomous agricultural status. There is some truth to this, but it is not the whole story.

Domestic life undergoes change in the course of years. The membership changes with the births, deaths, marriages, departures, return of persons; and membership also changes with respect to the peculiar statuses of persons at different ages, varying also with regard to their sex, ability, and related criteria. By viewing domestic arrangements at different points in time during a household's existence, one sees a cyclical development in the kinds of change in organization and composition.

We may view Mapuche domestic units in terms of three principle types: *elementary, joint-extended,* and *compound.* This is merely an analytic device for simplification, not an expression of all possible variations in living conditions.

A few highlights of the history of domestic organization in Mapucheland will throw light on the contemporary situation on the reservations, and will be of help in attempting to gauge the extent and depth of persistence and change involved. First, a brief definition of these family types.

Elementary family, as used in this case study, means one composed of husband and wife and their children. It is also possible to refer to incomplete elementary family households, consisting of less than the full complement suggested—for example, those in which either one of the spouses is lacking or in which there are no children. The vast majority of elementary family households in Mapucheland have the full complement of membership. Alonqueo's household, at the time of the author's arrival was an incomplete extended family. After his marriage it began to take on the features of a joint-extended family household, and after the birth of his child would have been a three-generation, joint-extended family household.

An *extended family* is one which has two adult generations, such as father, mother, and married son(s). This might be called a two-generation extended family; if there are also grandchildren, it is a three-generation extended family. It is a joint extended family if it includes married sons of the paterfamilias. If Alonqueo's brother had married and all of them lived in the same house it would have been a full-fledged joint-extended family household. It became so after Alonqueo's brother married, in 1955, and fathered two children. It completed another phase of the domestic cycle when Alonqueo died in 1959 and his wife moved back to her parents' house. The interpersonal relationships within extended families are more complex than within an elementary family. The Mapuche houses, many of which are over fifty years old, have seen the going and coming of different family types and have continued to endure, awaiting further cycles of domestic development.

The *compound family* is one in which there are half-siblings, a not uncommon feature in Mapucheland. This kind of family usually results from the paterfamilias having two or more wives, as in the case of Pablo, the uncle of Huenchemil. It may also occur outside the polygynous context, when a man or woman remarries after the death of the original spouse and procreates children in the new marriage.

Significant changes have taken place in family composition on the reservations since their founding. A comparison of old reservation maps with new ones indicates domiciliary changes; comparison of house-by-house censuses between then and now indicate changes in household composition. The accompanying Table 1, made up for five reservations on which I worked and for which there was good historical information, illustrates this point.

TABLE 1
NUMERICAL CHANGE IN THE COMPOSITION OF MAPUCHE FAMILIES

Reservation	Elementary		Extended		Compound	
	ca. 1900	1953	1900	1953	1900	1953
1	7	19	9	4	7	2
2	4	13	3	3	—	—
3	1	12	5	1	—	—
4	5	16	8	5	1	2
5	1	5	1	2	1	1

Today there is no advantage, military or other, in several families occupying a single house. The threat of attack has long passed, certain cooperative ventures have diminished in frequency and, in any event, there is sufficient spatial contiguity of households on the reservations for extended-family cooperation to be arranged easily enough. In addition, the separate domiciles reduce tension and friction between members of the larger family, especially between inmarried women and their mother-in-law. Polygyny, according to former accounts and genealogical investigation, has declined in most parts of Mapucheland. All of these changes are understandable to some extent in terms of ecological adjustments made in the context of reservation life, as are the threads of continuity and change in domestic organization.

Family Interrelationships: Husband and Wife

A husband and wife divide their labors so that the man takes care of the most arduous tasks outside the house and the woman most chores indoors. The husband performs almost all the chores directly connected with farming but the wife helps with the harvest, as needed, and winnows wheat and beans before they are stored in the family's wooden bins. If the husband needs another man's help, and does not have grown sons, he calls upon his father or brother to assist him, in a small-scale mingaco arrangement, or else looks to another relative with whom he may work vuelta mano, as described in Chapter 3.

During its early years, until children are old enough to perform adult work, the elementary family household is more dependent on relatives than it will be in later years. Alonqueo and his brother always worked together, although Alonqueo also occasionally worked in a *vuelta mano* arrangement with one of his younger uncles. Huenchemil, who had small children and a rather extensive holding, had major tasks such as plowing, seeding, and harvesting done by large-scale *mingaco*. Since he was the chief, nearly all of the households on his reservation felt obligated to accept his invitation, and because of his popularity, gladly put in a day's work for him. However, for smaller jobs, Huenchemil depended on one or two young cousins who received no more than a good meal for their work. Older men, such as Huenchemil's uncle, Pablo, farmed largely without outside help, since they had enough grown sons to assist them with most agricultural tasks.

It is not uncommon for a man and his wife to call one another kompang, the Araucanianized word for the Spanish compañero, which sets the tone of husband-wife relationships. A woman greatly influences her husband's decisions about farming and managing the family's affairs, even though the husband is unquestionably the boss of the household. We have also seen, in Alonqueo's case, how a widow continues to exercise control over her grown sons.

Mother and Children: The mother, in this otherwise patriarchal setting, is the principal disciplinarian and guardian of her children up to the time of their nubility. Since most of a girl's training consists of helping her mother with such tasks as household chores, gardening, and washing clothing in a nearby river or stream, a girl remains in close association with her mother until the time of her

Home life in Alonqueo's house. From left: his mother, author's wife, his sister, Alonqueo.

marriage. Boys, though, receive training from their father or older brother once they have reached puberty or have grown strong enough to do man's work.

Although often scolded—by the mother rather than the father—children are rarely physically punished. They may be punished for laziness by having extra chores heaped on them or by being left behind to guard the house and animals when the family goes on a visit or makes a trip to town. There is little difference in the manner in which boys and girls are either punished or rewarded until they reach their sub-teens, at which time boys are pretty much taken over by their father and treated, as nearly as possible, as men.

On the whole, growing children seem to want to meet their parents' expectations of them and attempt to perform like adults. The Mapuche parent tends to be lenient and permissive.

Father and Children: When a boy is considered old enough to receive instruction in agricultural work and general manly deportment, he comes almost entirely under the supervision of his father. He no longer performs household chores as his sisters do, but accompanies his father or elder brothers to the fields, to market, and so forth. He hears man's talk and strives to imitate the men around him. He might even supervise his sisters and younger brothers in the performance of their chores, especially when they are tending the flock of sheep, pasturing the cows and oxen, and so forth.

At about the age of fifteen, the boy, under the guidance of his father or other elders of the sublineage, begins to assume a young man's role in agriculture. He is entrusted with more responsibility, such as being left by himself to complete the plowing or harrowing of a section of the family fields, or to curry the horses, or to deliver in the ox-cart some sacks of grain or potatoes to a store, a neighbor's house, and so on. In these activities he is appraised and counselled by his father and by his elder brothers; he is judged as manly or not, as a good farmer or as an indifferent one.

In this strongly patrilineal society the relationship between father and son is of great organizational significance; that between father and daughter much less so. In his sons a man sees the continuation of his line, the perpetuation of his own heritage, and the propitiation of his ancestral spirits when he dies. Fathers and sons live together for life on the reservation of their birth and form a core unit in all activities connected with their household(s) and the reservation community. Daughters move off their reservation upon marriage and, ideally, live out their lives on their husband's reservation, among affinal kinsmen who are the lineage mates of their husbands, sons, and daughters.

Siblings: Brothers and sisters are treated much the same during their very early years, playing and working together under the eyes of their mother. As they reach puberty, however, they tend to have less activities in common, each beginning to prepare for adult life in different ways and under different tutelage. Brothers remain together for life on the same reservation and, if not in the same household, often in a compound of houses on paternal land. Brothers and sisters separate when the girls marry and go to live on their husband's reservation, but they enjoy a close and sympathetic relationship for life, which is of great structural importance in the marriage system. Sisters, under the traditional marriage pattern, may well reside together after marriage on the same reservation if they marry brothers or patrilineal kinsmen. If they marry men from different reservations, however, they see one another only occasionally at family reunions, funerals, fertility rites, and so forth.

Socialization of Children

Mapuche children are monolingual in Araucanian for the first six to nine years or so of their lives and are jokingly referred to as "old people," who generally speak little or no Spanish. The Mapuche tend to feel somewhat ashamed because they do not ordinarily speak Spanish and are often ridiculed by Chileans for their poor or "hard" accent. After more than 400 years of contact with Europeans, the Mapuche continue to use Araucanian as the language of the home, the reservation, and the Mapuche world—both natural and supernatural. This linguistic feature is of great importance in understanding how children are brought up, how Mapuche culture is perpetuated, and how traditional values are inculcated in the young people. The preservation of Araucanian reinforces Mapuche values, denies Chilean values with which these conflict, and shores up Mapuche social organization. Of course, monolingualism, even bilingualism to the extent that it exists, limits the alternatives to reservation life open to the Mapuche, symbolizing as it does an incompetence to adjust easily to Chilean culture and society. The very problems monolingualism creates operate as a conservative force among the Mapuche.

The child is exposed to this linguistic confinement. The Catholic missions fail to communicate easily with Mapuche because their values are well established during the first decade of their life. The reservation schools forbid the use of Araucanian, not only in the classroom but on the playground, recognizing that monolingualism, even bilingualism, presents a serious obstacle to the acculturation of the Mapuche.

The Mapuche child grows up surrounded by men and women who wear distinctive clothing, eat traditional food prepared in Mapuche style, and live in extended-family arrangements with numerous relatives whom he classifies in a manner totally different from Chileans. The child calls its mother and the other married women of the compound or extended family by the same kinship term. Father and father's brothers are also called by the same term. It is not that these persons cannot be distinguished linguistically, since they can be and are when the occasion calls for such distinctions to be made. The important thing is that usually it is not necessary to make such distinctions, thus reinforcing the notion of the residential unit, in which kinsmen are lumped according to their sex and generational membership and not ordinarily sorted out as persons. These are the people who scurry back and forth between houses, carrying steam-food from one to the other, borrowing and returning tools and other implements, and so on. The women winnow grain together, spin and weave together, and sometimes even take turns suckling each other's infants. These families gather in the night for long conversations around an open fire, for drinking bouts when drink is available. They separate to sleep in their respective quarters, but they may well work together in the fields the next day or do together whatever work has to be done.

There are always elderly persons in such households, persons who are grandparents to all the youngsters, who spend much of their time playing with the children, instructing them indirectly through stories of the good old days and by reinforcing the moral values of Mapuche society—all of course in the Araucanian language. The growing child is deeply affected by the communal life which is quite different from that in which the Chilean is raised.

Rural Chilean children are naive about city life but to a much less degree than Mapuche children. Chileans, even those of the peasant class, almost always visit relatives in towns and cities and become aware of "luxuries" not ordinarily enjoyed at home on the farm. Not so, as a rule, with Mapuche.

My wife had an interesting experience along these lines one day when she took a young girl from our reservation for an outing in the city of Temuco. Manuela had been to Temuco a number of times with her brothers, usually once or twice a year when they took wheat to the mill for grinding. However, Manuela had never been in anyone's house in town nor had she ever been to a movie, gone to a hotel, and so forth. She once had been taken to lunch by her brothers in a barroom which served Mapuche and which was in the shanty-town part of the city.

My wife took her directly to a missionary's house, where the mail was received and where some of our belongings were stored. It was assumed immediately that Manuela was our servant, a notion which we were never able to dispel fully. Nevertheless, Manuela ate a mid-morning snack in the kitchen and was greatly impressed by the sink with running hot and cold water, the refrigerator, the gas stove, and so on. When my wife was getting ready to leave, Manuela excused herself and went into the garden behind some bushes to relieve herself. Later she remarked with some surprise that it was too bad the Americans had no outhouse.

Manuela was also taken to a pension we occasionally stayed in and invited her to lunch. Manuela was not able to use the knife and fork but managed quite well with the spoon which is the principal utensil used by the Mapuche. After lunch, my wife acquainted her with the flush toilet and also showed her how the bathtub and shower worked. Manuela was a bit startled by the flush-toilet and could not understand why it was indoors.

On the street, Manuela had her first glimpse of store window displays in the better part of town and she marveled at the full counters, the many kinds of canned goods, and so forth. She also had her first ice cream cone and her first visit to a motion picture.

Manuela talked about her adventure day after day upon returning to the reservation. We took her and one of her brothers to town with us occasionally after that. Just before leaving Mapucheland for the United States, we returned to say goodbye to Manuela and her family. We were told that Manuela was working in Temuco as a house servant and that she was attending a vocational school in the evenings.

Working for Wages

An aspect of domestic organization which is becoming increasingly important is employment of one or more of the family members off the reservation. In almost all cases, these absentees (temporary or permanent) send money "home." In any event, their absence signifies a change in domestic life.

Largely because of over-crowding on the reservations, many young people emigrate to Chilean farms and cities each year, some even crossing the Andes to look for work in Argentina. As stated earlier, there are several avenues open to Mapuche, most of which lead irrevocably to such jobs as the army, national police force, semiskilled trades and manual labor on haciendas and in cities, and for girls, domestic service and prostitution.

Mapuche are Chilean nationals. If they are able to read and write they receive an identity card which entitles them to vote in all elections. Mapuche males must also serve a year as conscripts in the army. Most return to the reservations after this experience. Many, however, remain in the ranks. Those who return sometimes find that their expected inheritance of land is not forthcoming, or that other things have changed. Having tasted life off the reservations, some of these young men yearn for more. They may reenter the army or apply for admission to the national police force. Several thousand Mapuche are probably employed by the army or police force, distributed from Arica to Punta Arenas.

There are also several semiskilled trades which seem to attract Mapuche men to the cities. One is the baking industry, which employs Mapuche at the less specialized jobs. The other is the transportation industry, which employs Mapuche as bus drivers and taxicab operators. Both of these skills are taught in the army.

The transition from independent farmer to employee on a Chilean hacienda (fundo) is an easy one, and of seasonal duration in most cases. Still, there are more and more Mapuche who settle as peons on Chilean haciendas or who leave for work on Argentine ranches and farms across the Andes, sometimes returning as comparative strangers to the reservations of their birth many years after abandoning reservation life. Whether ditch-digger, cowboy, or farmhand, the Mapuche is still an *indio*, member of *otra raza*. It is a stigma which does not easily wash off, one which makes for very limited economic alternatives off the reservation, limiting most Mapuche to the lowest rung of the social ladder.

As for women, their alternatives are even more restricted than those of the men. In a country with few modern conveniences, even in most of the middle-income city homes, and with a tradition of domestic servitude, there are many openings for reservation girls in Chilean households. Also the brothels of Chilean cities have many Mapuche girls; especially girls of mixed (Mapuche and Chilean) parentage, born in the slums, without much hope, without much education, without much understanding of their heritage, resenting illegitimacy, and resorting to prostitution. Even so, if their number reaches 3,000 in all, they represent but one percent of the total Mapuche population.

10

Political Life

MAPUCHE POLITICAL LIFE may be illustrated by considering two of its principal aspects. On the one hand there is chieftainship, which flourishes under a communal localism fostered by the reservation system; on the other there is the factor of universal suffrage, which involves Mapuche as individuals in national and regional political issues. While these two areas are complementary, the latter may be viewed as an alternative to traditional political life.

Prereservation Times

Historical accounts of prereservation Mapuche political life have been summarized succinctly by Father John Cooper in the following excerpt:

> Some major features of the system . . . are quite clear. There was no peacetime over-all chief, no centralization of authority. . . . Furthermore, such authority as was invested in kinship heads and local "chiefs" was very limited—exclusively or almost exclusively consultative and persuasive, with little or no coercive power. They had no recognized rights to inflict punishment, to claim tribute or personal service, or to demand obedience from their kinsfolk or "subjects." The latter paid no attention to them and did as they pleased if the leaders showed themselves arrogant or domineering.
>
> Decisions regarding peacetime affairs and warlike undertakings were usually made in conference of the responsible men and subheads at the house or meeting-ground of the head or "chief" after free expression of views and by common agreement. There was a certain loose hierarchy of honor and status (rather than authority proper) embracing higher and lower heads and "chiefs"—which brings us to the less clear features of the . . . sociopolitical structure.
>
> In the course of time, particularly after the beginning of the 19th century, a certain increase in the executive and judicial power and authority accrued to peace time headmen . . . and the earlier atomistic peace-time political structure assumed somewhat greater unity, cohesion, and hierarchization. But the basic democratic forms and functions persisted largely intact.

In continuation, Cooper wrote:

The chief crimes recognized were adultery and wife-stealing, murder, theft, homicidal sorcery, and treason. The offended party and his kin dealt with the offender; in earlier times headmen and other caciques had little or no authority to try cases or to pronounce judgment. Adultery, murder, and sorcery were punishable by death, and sometimes were actually so punished; but more commonly in cases of adultery and murder, composition was resorted to with payment of strings of llanka [beads] . . .

The Reservation Period

Beginning with the mapping and administration of more than 3000 small reservations, the Chilean government created an equal number of Mapuche chiefs and gave them legal recognition. The vast majority of these chiefs also received recognition in Mapuche customary law (admapu).

We have already seen how chiefs organized labor on the reservations. The new chiefs' authority was much more than consultative and persuasive, as Cooper described for an earlier period. Chiefs did claim tribute, in the form of gifts from household heads on their reservation and they demanded and received personal service.

Chilean law forbade movement from one reservation to another in the frontier zone, and the creation of fixed farming entities, to which only the chief had title, redefined the role and status of chief in the political as well as in the economic sphere.

Chiefs came to have life and death powers over their constituents. Social grievances were usually framed in terms of witchcraft and witches were dismembered and burned under the most adverse conditions. Otherwise, they, along with other trouble-makers, were evicted from the reservation precincts. Eviction still occurs today and is sometimes forced by beatings at the behest of the chief.

Since chiefs controlled the allocation of land on the reservations, they also came to have control over marriage and postmarital residence. If marriage were disapproved by the chief, allotment of land was withheld from the young man; consequently he either refrained from marrying or was forced to leave the reservation to do so. Today, the chief's authority in matters of marriage and residence can be activated if the young man's father or other adult relative seeks the chief's intervention in preventing the marriage from taking place. It is usually not necessary to go to such lengths since the de facto control of land and, therefore, the economic basis for marriage, is worked out within the framework of sublineage organization.

Two main features of the land question are important in understanding the development of chieftainship on the reservations. One is that which concerns population pressure on limited reservation land and the other is the disbanding of reservations under the policy of división. Population pressure increased gradually in the first decades of the reservation system, not only as population grew but as productivity of agriculture diminished. Pressure for division of reservation land assumed great proportions in the early part of the twentieth century, before the

Mapuche had time to make firm adjustments to reservation life. Since the 1920s, however, *división* has decreased markedly, having almost come to a standstill.

After the reservation policy of 1884 went into effect, a one-eighth clause of land division was combined with a special inducement to chiefs, who were to receive more land than ordinary Mapuche, to work for division. The one-eighth clause stipulated that upon petition of one-eighth of the households, the reservation would be disbanded and the land be given in severalty title (in one's own right) to household heads. In this way the Chilean government hoped to stimulate a general movement in favor of abandoning reservation life. Once more, a good deal of land was lost to the Mapuche.

Then things changed: the Mapuche resisted disbandment of their reservation communities. This turn of events is signalized by the government's continued attempt to modify the division clause so as to appeal to individual Mapuche and bypass the authority of the chiefs. In 1927 the law was changed again, so that all that was necessary for division was the appeal of a single household on any reservation. Finally, after even this measure failed, the government decreed that even this single vote was not necessary and that it could disband reservations at its own discretion—which it did on a small scale where land was claimed as public domain in the frontier zone.

In 1931 the law was once more remodeled so that one-third of the households of a reservation were needed to vote for division. This does not indicate a marked change in the long-range policy of the Chilean government, however, as indicated by the law which passed the National Congress in 1960 providing for the gradual disbandment of reservations. The political future of the reservations is uncertain as of this writing.

Chieftainship Today

Huenchemil is the son and grandson of chiefs, and an able and respected middle-aged man. Although not the oldest man of his lineage, he is considered the most important elder. He knows a good deal of the intricacies of Chilean politics and, therefore, is highly respected as a political leader, not only on his own reservation but also on surrounding reservations, whose chiefs frequently ask his advice about political matters. Furthermore, Huenchemil knows religious ritual and takes an important part in agricultural fertility ceremonies. He is not as knowledgeable in ritual and prayer as some of the older men on his and other reservations, but people feel that his other qualities compensate for this. Besides, Huenchemil is receptive to advice from older men, which helps ingratiate him with all of his constituents and enhances his reputation in the general region. It is interesting to note that his relative lack of ritual skills results from the fact that his older brother was being groomed to succeed to the father's position as chief, kinship leader, and ritual priest of the reservation. With his brother's death, Huenchemil came into line but was many years behind in this traditional sort of training.

In most respects, Huenchemil is a typical, or average, chief. He speaks occasionally of descending from a noble Mapuche family and once in a while, mainly for the benefit of his sons, talks about Mapuche military prowess before the time of reservations. One hears statements of this sort from chiefs and other important men on almost all reservations. It forms part of the past of which they are very proud and recounting it seems to serve as a kind of buffer to the problems and pains of contemporary life.

Today's chief does not have legal title to reservation land according to Chilean law. Reservation law made no provision for the transfer of such title from the original chief of the newly formed reservation to his heirs. Nevertheless, the good chief is accorded both *de facto* and *de jure* rights to reservation land according to *admapu*, Mapuche customary law. So strong is the notion that chiefs own all the land on the reservation that even Chileans who have dealings with ordinary Mapuche (harvesting and threshing wheat, working half-shares, and so forth) seek out the permission of the reservation chief to do so.

The Chief is still symbolic head of large-scale cooperative ventures on the reservation, such as ox-road and bridge repairs, land-clearing, house-building, and even large-scale preparation or harvesting of fields. His organizational role, however, has diminished since early reservation times. Huenchemil told me that he, for example, was always informed whenever important reservation activities were in the offing and was invited to take part, and that he felt obligated to put in an appearance, partake of the food and drink, and so forth. He said that the people did not need him to organize their activities, with the exception of the agricultural fertility ceremony, because they knew well enough what to do.

Because of the growing importance of sublineages, the chief now heads up an informal council of elders who are in turn the heads of these lineage branches. In delegating some authority and responsibility to these elders, the chief firms up his own position *vis á vis* the community. This is·especially true in the delegation of religious responsibility at the time of the fertility ceremonies.

While perhaps not as effective a political spokesman of his new, more complex community as previously, the chief is nevertheless successor to chiefs and is a focal point on his own reservation. If he is a good chief, that is, if he has ability and grace in ritual matters, is wise and honest, and has a strong personality, he carries much political weight on the reservation. For example, he may be able to dissuade a faction from pressing for *división*, even though the faction is legally large enough to appeal to the government for the reservation to be remapped and divided into severalty holdings. A traditionally oriented chief, one who helps the community keep peace with its neighbors and its ancestors, has much at stake in keeping his reservation a functioning unit, and those who follow him are mainly kinsmen who share this interest.

Alternatives to Traditional Political Organization

I do not see any short term alternatives to traditional leadership on the reservations. Occasional bits of information which trickle down to me from Chilean friends indicate that chieftainship has remained essentially as I came to know it in 1953. Reservations continue to resist division, which speaks for a certain minimum of community integration around the secular and religious leadership expressed in daily life on the reservations. It is probable nevertheless that the Mapuche will strike a new balance in their relationships with the Chilean government and come more and more into the sphere of governmental agencies. These agencies have characteristically dealt with Mapuche as individual citizens— albeit of special reservation status—and have attempted to by-pass customary chieftainship. This would seem to be the long-range trend in Mapucheland, but its actual course is uncertain.

Alternatives to chieftainship may be viewed in regard to problems of an intersocietal nature between Mapuche and Chileans. Of greatest importance here is the land question, and specifically, the policy of the abandonment *versus* the preservation of the reservation system. As we have tried to show, chieftainship has undergone modification since the reservation system went into effect. It first developed strongly, experiencing a phase in which the newly created reservation chiefs constituted the sole spokesmen for their communities in all relations with Chileans and other Mapuche. Since that time many chiefs no longer mediate effectively between their reservations (or individuals on them) and Chileans (agencies, courts, banks, and individuals). Part of the authority which chiefs have relinquished has been assumed by what may be called Mapuche pressure groups. Chiefs continue to exercise great authority in inter- and intrareservational matters. But the political pressure groups express more enlightened or sophisticated opinion and policy, and seem more and more to be relied on by the Mapuche (including chiefs) in joint policy *vis á vis* the Chilean government and its agencies in political matters of a regional, pan-Mapuche nature.

There is ample evidence to show that where traditional political leadership is weak, political conditions are most volatile with respect to Chilean-Mapuche relationships. As always, there is an economic (land) basis to the dispute, and action takes the form either of violent or crafty dispossession of the land. Recent Chilean newspaper articles (mainly in left-wing papers during April, 1965) testify to the persistence of this condition.

Several groups of Mapuche "occupied" a few Chilean haciendas (fundos) and laid claim to the land on the basis of their "immemorial right" as well as appealing to the government to implement the recent Chilean Agrarian Reform project. They were armed with old rifles and spears. According to the reports there was no bloodshed and the Mapuche were driven off by Chilean troops.

It is interesting to note that these "uprisings," as they are described in the newspapers, took place in the northern, most highly acculturated part of Mapucheland, where chieftainship is weakest and where communal reservation life has deteriorated. Photographs suggest that the Mapuche leaders were organizers of the pressure groups, men wearing *fedoras* (felt hats) and topcoats in contrast to the poncho-wearing *indio*, bare-headed or with his broad-brimmed *huaso* hat.

When the author was doing fieldwork among the Mapuche, the two most important pressure groups were Corporación Araucana and Unión Araucana. They supported different aspects of issues involving reservation land and the system in general. The Corporación opposed the policy of división and the Unión favored a modified version of it. Then as now (according to my latest personal communications) the two groups were in fact in sympathy with regard to improving the Mapuche way of life, differing mainly in their opinion of the best means of achieving such uplifting.

The Corporación and the Unión are roughly a half century old. I suspect they have failed to achieve startling results for two main reasons. One is the recalcitrance of the Chilean government and a general antagonism to the Mapuche and the reservation system. The other is the conservatism of the Mapuche themselves. Mapuche distrust politicians, even fellow Mapuche. All things point to the fact that political life goes on pretty much as I came to know it on the reservations more than a decade ago.

I believe that those reservations having good ritual leadership and functioning ritual congregations present a solid front to political innovation, and changes will continue to take place very slowly. Traditional leadership must be revamped, however, to meet todays needs. It seems very likely that the influence of specific pressure groups (some new ones have emerged since 1953) will wax and wane. These are organizational changes which, nevertheless, do not immediately affect the structure of Mapuche politics.

11

Gods and the Afterworld

L IKE MANY other primitive people, the Mapuche have their own gods, their own eternal rewards, their own sense of damnation and sin. Their cosmological notions have certainly withstood the test of time, remaining relatively unchanged during more than 400 years of contact with whites and formal missionization. These beliefs, and the rituals associated with them, provide the Mapuche with a formidable bastion against radical cultural and social change, and serve to sanction the traditional way of life.

Names and Attributes of the Gods

Mapuche gods are described as old people who are invisible and who have rather specific and limited powers. The deities comprise sets of husbands and wives who have children; but, for the Mapuche, the male gods and the male offspring of certain of these are of greatest importance and are attributed the greatest powers. There is a hierarchical framework of divinity which closely parallels the patrilineal and generational concepts of the Mapuche.

Heading the hierarchy of the pantheon is *ñenechen*. His apical position may be a reflection of Christian influence on Mapuche thinking. However, noted anthropologists have argued against this view and, in the absence of solid evidence to the contrary, I feel that Christian influence has been minimal. There is, however, much evidence indicating that strong influences from the Incas had emanated from Peru in pre-Spanish times.

Inca religion, for example, stressed increasing the food supply and curing supernatural illness. Divination was such an important prerequisite to religious activity that the influence of a priesthood on public affairs was very great. Sin and purification were important concepts and sacrifice accompanied nearly every religious act.

The Inca had a larger number of supernatural beings of varying power

Shaman beating kultrun during a curing rite.

and importance. *Viracocha*, the Creator of all other supernatural beings, and men, ruled them much as the Inca Emperor ruled the empire. He was represented as a man and there were statues of him in a number of temples. Although the Mapuche conceive of their ñenechen as masculine also, they have never reified him or built temples of worship.

The lesser supernatural beings of the Inca earned greatest respect among the Mapuche: Sun, Moon, Thunder, Stars, Earth, and Sea. According to Inca belief, virtuous persons went to live with the Sun and the other celestial beings. The Mapuche notions of life after death reflect Inca cosmology. Sacrificial beings, mainly animals among the Mapuche, had great importance. Strangulation, throat-cutting, emphasis on the palpitating heart, are still major features of Mapuche religious rites, whereas the millions of Quechuá-speaking Peruvians have long-since lost the aboriginal vitality of their ancient religion.

The Mapuche are a polytheistic people. Their many gods may be classified as major, minor, and lesser deities having, respectively, ethnic (that is, total societal), regional, and lineage importance. Ñenechen is an active, interceding god but is not felt to be omniscient or omnipotent. Many Mapuche have learned of the omnipotence and omniscience of the white man's god and, discussing him with foreigners, will at times, as a defensive mechanism, attribute their gods the same qualities. Nevertheless, many of their chance remarks and the entire network of their beliefs indicate that ñenechen does not have the attributes of the Christian God.

Ultimate appeal is made to ñenechen to direct or control other deities, but these other deities and the forces of evil have considerable latitude of action. Missionaries are tempted to equate the forces of evil with Satan in his several guises, a logic which the Mapuche are able to understand but one to which they give no credence or at least no importance, considering the white man to be wrong.

Pillan is god of thunder or volcanoes and is a minor deity. There are also pillan who are familiar spirits of shamans. Considering shamans as witches, and equating volcanoes with fire and brimstone, Christian missionaries have elevated pillan to the stature of Satan; thus opposing ñenechen to pillan as God to Satan. The Mapuche do not let this affect their beliefs and rituals, however.

Ñenechen is the "god of the Mapuche" or "the ruler of the Mapuche" and is not confused by the vast majority of Mapuche with the white man's god. There is also a creator and ruler of earth, called *ñenemapun*, who is sometimes identified with ñenechen. In addition, there is *elchen* who is regarded as "maker of the people" and when called *elchen chau* is considered the "father of the people." Sometimes ñenemapun and elchen chau are equated with ñenechen but most often they are not. From the Mapuche view there is nothing illogical about the creator of earth, creator of people, and ruler of the people being three distinct deities.

The minor gods control specific phenomena and usually are identified with these. The most important of the minor gods, judging from how frequently they are propitiated in public ritual and from the frequency of their mention in stories or myths, would seem to be: *pillan fucha* and his wifely counterpart *pillan kushe*, the god and goddess of thunder or volcanoes; *lafken fucha/lafken kushe*, god and goddess of the sea; *antü fucha/kushe*, god and goddess of the sun; *küyen fucha/*

kushe, god and goddess of the moon; *huilli fucha/kushe*, god and goddess of the south wind–and so forth.

Since "everything has its spirit" and thus, is controlled by a deity, all classes of animal, vegetable, and inorganic substances (for example, "sky stones," meteors, planets, stars, and so on) have their godly representations. Since Mapuche mention these deities only rarely, the ones previously cited appear to be the truly significant ones in terms of ritual observance. The others of course have their importance in Mapuche cosmology in rounding out the universe.

Although under the control of ñenechen, the minor gods have considerable force and freedom of action, and are described for the most part as capricious. Their activities, or force, must be channelled by proper propitiatory rites and, ultimately, recourse is made to ñenechen to oversee and direct their activities in behalf of mankind (that is, Mapuche). In turn, however, some of these minor gods are asked to intercede before ñenechen on behalf of mankind. This is especially true of *kupuka fucha* and *kupuka kushe*, god and goddess of abundance, and their sons, the *karuhua*.

One night I "saw" the *karuhua*! We were walking home, and had covered about three miles, when Alonqueo grabbed me by the arm and said, "Look there." Sure enough, there was an "object," a person, if you will. It was in fact a luminescent tree stump in a bog, but the suggestion, after drinking wine for several hours that evening, was sufficient to convince *everyone* that we were at grips with the supernatural. When we arrived home and had told the story of our encounter to Alonqueo's mother, brother, and sisters, all of them began telling stories of similar encounters. This added credence to our story, which was told over and over during the rest of my residence. The crop was very poor that year, and the supernatural encounter was interpreted as the *karuhua's* attempt to tell us that the wheat crop would fail and that other (unspecified) means should be taken to fill the family larder.

There is some indication in the literature about the Mapuche—although little or none in oral histories—that ñenechen and the minor gods were prayed to to grant the Mapuche military prowess and also to lessen the dire effects of continual skirmishing with whites. Today most attention is given in public ritual to the agricultural needs of the Mapuche, and the gods and ancestors are asked to care for the general well-being of the people by granting abundant harvests, increase of animals, and good health. These prayers deal in detail with the kinds of weather most suitable to current needs, the kinds of crops to be grown, and so on. Thunder, which symbolizes rain and devastating earthquakes (volcanoes) is "controlled" through the propitiation of pillan fucha or *tralkan fucha*, as he is sometimes called and, if to no avail, then recourse is made to ñenechen to control this force to the best interest of mankind. Similarly with the northwind, the southwind, the sun and the moon, and with all forces and phenomena. The setting for communication between the Mapuche and their gods is the great agricultural fertility ceremony, *ñillatun*, which will be described in Chapter 15.

The hierarchical nature of divinity and the progression from man to divinity, central to Mapuche thought, is clearly seen in the connecting role of ancestral chiefs (*lonko*). Chiefs' spirits walk with the sons of the gods. In most of Mapucheland the most important among the sons of the gods are the karuhua, mentioned above, who walk the earth benefitting mankind. Their activities are directed or channelled by ancestral chiefs whose interest, while ideally pan-Mapuche, is in fact focused on regional or local populations. These chiefs are essentially mythical ancestors of the Mapuche who have become regional deities in some instances. Their attributes are synthetic creations of the Mapuche mind and reflect Mapuche concepts of valor, responsibility, and authority with respect to chiefly status and progression to deity. This takes us directly to a consideration of all ancestral spirits and the place they hold in Mapuche ideas about the supernatural.

Ancestors' Spirits

Central to Mapuche religious belief is the concept of ancestral spirits. The most important of these are their former chiefs—those elders, lineage founders, military leaders, who walk the earth in the company of the sons of the gods. In genealogical reckoning there is a convergence upon the lineage founder, the apical ancestor, the lineage deity.

Huenchemil's father and grandfather were such men, and he often spoke to me about his "noble" ancestry and how his forebears were becoming deities. The propitiated spirits of fathers and grandfathers were not automatically divine. There was a maturation period involved, during which the spirits had to do good for the people, along with the karuhua, and had to prove themselves to the people through their good actions.

Luís, being a Christian convert, merely told me that Mapuche chiefs believed that their ancestors were gods. Luís was strongly opposed to this belief and called it a manifestation of witchcraft, which was completely out of line with Mapuche reasoning. Alonqueo believed ancestors became gods but, to his regret, the people on his reservation did not believe strongly enough to help preserve the traditional religion. Alonqueo pointed out that the old religion was dying and that Christianity was unattractive to the Mapuche; it was the religion of "milky white" people who couldn't speak Araucanian and who also had difficulty speaking and understanding Spanish. This was almost entirely an expression of distaste for North American Protestant missionaries rather than criticism of Chilean Catholics, who were tolerated by the Mapuche.

Spirits of ordinary ancestors may be active in the affairs of the living. If they are, however, it is often because their spiritual heirs have failed in some ritual obligation toward them. Whatever the case may be, the spirits who return to Mapucheland from the haven of the dead run the risk of contamination by a sorcerer-witch (*kalku*), and are, therefore, a threat to the well-being of the living. Indeed, during the first part of the funeral ceremony, there is a special activity called *amulpellun* which consists of the encirclement of the precincts in which the corpse is displayed (during the wake) and which is designed to drive away the evil spirits. This ceremony may be repeated on occasions when there is evidence of spirit return, even long after burial, in order to permit the ancestral visitor to depart without danger of contact with the forces of evil.

The dead are pictured as living abundant and easy lives in a shadow world where they carry on traditional activities. This afterworld is sometimes called *nomelafken*, which places it across the Pacific Ocean, and sometimes *wenumapu*, the land above. The former seems to be used more along the coast and the latter in parts of the Central Valley and the Andean uplands, although both terms are known to all Mapuche. The Mapuche do not see any disagreement in these two designations, which it is said refer to the same place. There is only one proper abode of the dead. Christian influence is possibly responsible for another designation, *kutralmapu*, or fireland, which a few Mapuche claim to be a stopping place of the spirit on its way to the final resting place. The concepts of Hell or Purgatory are foreign to Mapuche thought and imperfectly understood even by the few converts to Christianity.

While ancestral spirits (excepting those of former chiefs) should remain at rest in the afterworld, they occasionally return to earth. The sets of rights and obligations which bind together the living and their ancestors are jeopardized when this happens, and their return is most often interpreted to mean that the living have failed to satisfy their obligation to the dead.

Although the dead are invisible, they may appear in dreams or may make their presence known by moving household objects, making noises, and so forth. Ancestors are beneficent spirits and are not themselves feared. They mostly return to earth to warn their heirs of impending danger or to offer help (finding lost or stolen objects seems paramount in this regard). Danger results, as stated, from a supernatural disequilibrium due to ritual inadequacy—in short, because of some failure to deactivate the forces of evil through proper care of ancestral and other divine beings. Ancestral spirits may reveal death to their relatives, depending on their interpretation of dreams or spirit presence. In extreme cases, the person in fear of death will consult a shaman (*machi*), either to make sure the visiting spirit does not fall into the hands of a witch (*kalku*) or to perform certain ritual acts to protect the threatened person himself from contamination.

Alonqueo's family, with the exception of his mother, were fairly sophisticated. Alonqueo and his brother were thought of locally as "good Indians," which meant that they were reasonably progressive farmers and spoke good Spanish. Their fear of the *wüthwüth* (bird of evil omen), however, was known in the vicinity of their reservation and was taken to be a sign of their paganism by local Chilean peasants. This meant little to me until the actual appearance of a wüthwüth one night.

Alonqueo and I had returned from Temuco in the late afternoon. His brother had also gone to town that day but had not been with us. The brothers were both dressed in their patched blue serge suits and were wearing white shirts, ties, shoes, and socks. This heightened the impression of sophistication just mentioned.

The evening meal was being prepared. Alonqueo and I were sipping *mate* (Paraguayan tea) and nibbling on the freshly baked bread. The old lady, Alonqueo's mother, and my wife were drinking wine which we had brought from town.

After dinner the Alonqueo family became tense, for no reason I could observe. The setting was important. The fact we three men were dressed in suits, and so forth, was unusual in the plank-walled, thatch-roofed house. The unusual quality accentuated what happened next.

Suddenly, Alonqueo, his brother, mother, and two sisters rushed out of the house into the pitch black night. Some of them carried fire brands with them. My wife and I followed them out, wondering what the trouble was. There was a muttering of "wüthwüth, wüthwüth," and they threw the firebrands at the huge oak tree outside the house. The bird of evil omen was in the tree, and with the fire and noise, flew away.

An actual bird flew away, they told me, called wüthwüth. I have seen such birds in daytime; they exist. They are considered birds of evil omen mainly after sundown, or if they linger near one's house. The family rushed outside because they heard the call of the bird, which sounds (and I have heard this) somewhat like his name. I did not hear the call that night, however.

The Alonqueo family were really frightened by this event. The men, however, dissembled their fear and tried to calm the mother and girls. The old woman and the girls chatted all night about the event and referred to it now and again for weeks afterward.

Generally speaking, the Mapuche feel that their ancestors dwell together in the afterworld. There they are supposed to remain in eternal contentment, except for chiefs whose obligation involves looking after the well-being of the living. Chiefs, in company of the sons of the gods, are thus protected from the pitfalls of contamination to which ordinary ancestral spirits are exposed upon returning to earth. Chiefs look after the well-being of the living, not the dead, and the living in turn attend, through ritual and prayer, to the well-being of their ancestors. There is, then, an obvious linkage between the ancestral and contemporary Mapuche worlds, with the ancestral spirits constituting direct links between mortals and deities.

It is interesting to note that the notion of patrilineal descent is so pervasive that it is employed in linking mystical ancestors (who have ethnic or regional importance) to local groups of Mapuche, even though the Mapuche realize that genetic ties of relationship are impossible to determine. An example or two will indicate this.

As mentioned, the god of thunder, usually called pillan, is prayed to as an ancestral god in the Andean region of Mapucheland, where he is felt to be ancestral to several groups of reservations, or ritual congregations, in that general area. He is also known, but not conceived of as a lineal ancestor, by Mapuche who live along the coast. In the same manner, the god of the southwind is mythical ancestor to Mapuche groups who live along the Pacific coast, and is propitiated by most if not all reservations along the coast. He is known in the Andes but is considered a coastal deity. These are gross regional variations. There are even finer examples.

One of the Mapuche creation or origin-myths comes to mind here. It has to do with Manquian and it serves to show how a pan-Mapuche deity, *laf-kenche*, god of the sea, has been refracted into a local, generalized ancestor in one part of the coast. The story is roughly as follows.

Manquian was a shellfisher who lived long ago. He was in the water one day when his feet became stuck to two rocks. He felt that he could not free himself and called to people on shore to help him. Eventually they held a shamanistic performance to assist him. Still, he turned gradually to stone. The people believe that he is now a fisher of souls, lord of the sea, and that they are Manquian's "people." Manquian is a mythical local deity who is known only by rumor in much of the Central Valley and Andes. On the southern coast, however, he is tied to his "people" by kinship sentiments, rather than by genealogy, and is considered an important member of the pantheon.

There is a regional focus on certain deities known to all Mapuche and an overlapping in the propitiation of these mythical ancestors from one region to the next. I feel that this is a result of a gradation between actual, authentic ancestors and mythical ancestors in an ongoing process of full ancestral deification.

Forces of Evil

The sorcerer-witch or *kalku* is the embodiment of evil, although even she (most are women) may make herself invisible or transform herself into other forms. Her world is inhabited by numerous invisible forces of evil which may make themselves spectrally visible or even assume human guise. The Mapuche are deeply concerned with these malignant forces, especially obvious in time of stress, a concern which manifests itself both in their private, individual affairs and during public rituals, such as fertility rites and funeral ceremonies.

The Mapuche have a generic term, *wekufe*, which refers to all malevolent forces. Within this general classification it is possible to discern some of the most common evil forces; certain animal forms, natural phenomena, and ghosts. These wekufe by their own force or through the agency of a witch may remain either visible or invisible, or may assume any of the three general forms just mentioned. Mostly active at night, wekufe may also operate in daytime, and while most often under the control of a witch, they occasionally act independently, even to the point of killing the witch if her powers are not strong enough to protect her.

The animal forms assumed by wekufe are highly varied and are considered more or less dangerous depending on the circumstances in which they are observed. A few examples should suffice.

The most common forms are animals of the field and forest seen under unusual conditions—perhaps appearing in unexpected places and being somewhat distorted in shape or size. There are also wholly unnatural forms, such as the *chonchon*, a bird with a human head (that of the witch), or the *waillepen*, a large beast of the forest which is capable of taking the shape of a sheep or the combined features of a sheep and a cow. All are dangerous to mankind. They almost always suck their victim's blood and contaminate the victim, who, in turn, is in danger of becoming a blood-sucking ghost. Shamanistic counter-magic is the only recourse in such cases.

Another subcategory of wekufe, consisting of natural phenomena called *cherufe*, are fireballs, comets, shooting stars, whirlwinds, and many other such things. It is common belief that these phenomena are imbued with an evil spirit and may be controlled by a sorcerer-witch or that they may act randomly. Whatever the interpretation, the presence of these phenomena forbodes evil, suffering, and death in Mapucheland.

Although the Mapuche do not have a word which translates into English as "ghost," they nevertheless describe certain malevolent beings in a manner which corresponds somewhat to our concept of ghost. Ghosts are evil, contaminated ancestral spirits which have fallen under the power of a kalku. When spirits of the dead become contaminated, they cease being classed as ancestors and automatically are transformed into wekufe/ghosts.

The most common ghost forms, those observed most frequently and about which there are innumerable stories, are *witranalwe* and *anchimallen*, each of which assumes a human-like form when making its presence known to the living. Witranalwe are large figures, usually mounted on a huge horse which gallops over the highways and byways of Mapucheland. Anchimallen are child-sized, usually dressed in white or appearing luminescent. Witranalwe are ghosts of adults, anchimallen of children. Both are death-dealing, blood-sucking specters of the night. *Witranalwe* means "strange spirit" and *anchimallen* signifies a child-sized, usually luminescent, spirit. Both are abroad at night. *Witranalwe* tend to assume human form, although larger than life size, and have accentuated features, such as saucer-like eyes, huge teeth, large nose, and so forth. They are frequently seen astride a cavalry horse and dressed in a white or black tunic. Anchimallen are most often seen walking along the byways or through the woods and are described much like the luminscent, sheet-covered ghosts known to Europeans and North Americans.

Although they are both extremely dangerous ghosts, the witranalwe is always described in more fearsome terms than the anchimallen. He is large and ugly; he gallops along the roads at night; he is able to kill humans merely by being close to them. The anchimallen is less feared, perhaps because it is usually seen from a distance.

One dark night, while walking along the main road with Huenchemil and picking our way through mud holes, we were almost run down by a horseman. It was a nasty experience since we had to scramble in the mud to get out of the rider's way. I shouted after the rider but Huenchemil grabbed me by the arm and led the way home across the fields, hardly saying a word. When we arrived safely by his fireside, he explained at length that we had had a brush with a witranalwe. He told the story to other people the following day and soon the entire neighborhood was talking about it. In a day or so word reached us that several other Mapuche had seen the night rider farther up the Tolten River. It was assumed then that the witranalwe had left our region and there were expressions of relief.

12

Shamanism

I N THIS and the following chapter our attention will be focused on illness, personal misfortune, and death. For the Mapuche, these tragedies are conceived, not as natural events, but as supernaturally induced forces of evil embodied in the sorcerer-witch. These forces are combatted by the shaman and her familiar spirits. Illness, misfortune, and death are considered by the Mapuche to reflect chinks in their moral armor because they are thought to be the consequences of incorrect propitiation of ancestors and spirits. This thinking contributes to weaknesses in their social relationships and bring about additional stresses in them. In describing the roles of the shaman and the sorcerer-witch in affecting these relations, we deal with the subtle interaction of supernaturalism and social solidarity in its day-to-day dimensions on the reservations.

The Shaman's Art

The Mapuche dichotomize their supernatural world into the classic opposites of good and evil, consisting of both beings and activities. Shamans are associated with good; sorcerers connected with evil. The shaman is the curer *par excellence* and is continually concerned with right and wrong, good and evil. Almost every reservation has its own shaman or has access to the services of one on a nearby reservation.

Shamans must train for their profession, often for many years. They must learn special lore, songs, and techniques, such as the ability to induce trances, perform ventriloquism, diagnose illnesses, and make divination—all unknown to the ordinary Mapuche. Above all, they must have "power" (or the *appearance* of power) if they are to grapple successfully with the "supernatural" forces of evil. Their role in Mapuche society is, therefore, quite different from that of another important ritual functionary, the *ñillatufe* or ritual priest, who conducts the great agricultural fertility ceremony.

To assist them in the curing rites—called *machitun*—the shaman or *machi* has a set of paraphernalia reminiscent of that used by Siberian shamans. The two most prominent pieces of equipment employed by shamans are the shallow drum (*kultrun*) and the carved pole (*rewe*). The drum, beaten almost continuously in some ceremonies, helps induce a trance state; the step-notched pole, which the shaman sometimes climbs during ceremonies, is a sacred symbol of office fixed in the ground outside the shaman's house. The kultrun is made of a shallow wooden bowl, about eighteen inches in diameter, and covered by velum. The cover is often undecorated but sometimes carries a symbolic design of the Mapuche universe depicting four quarters of the world and its center. The notched rewe is frequently carved near the top in the form of a crude face, the significance of which is by no means clear. I have seen *rewe* carved with faces and woman's breasts and was told by the shamans who owned them that they represented *pillan* or familiar spirits, which would, of course, be those of ancestral shamans. (See cover also.)

Shamans use a specially made drumstick which also symbolizes their power, and some combination of gourd rattles and sleigh bells, also used at certain parts of almost every curing ceremony. The ritual consists of beating the drum over the patient's body and, shaking the rattles over him. Shamans also suck and massage the affected parts of their client's body, if this kind of treatment is indicated by the diagnosis, and may also blow tobacco smoke or pour—or spray—from their mouth medicinal water (made from various herbal concoctions depending upon the illness to be cured) over the sick person's body in the four cardinal directions of the compass.

Curing rites almost always take place indoors—in the shaman's house or that of the patient—where a fire, as an integral part of the paraphernalia, is used for light, for special lighting effects, or to burn tobacco, to heat and tighten the drumskin, and other assorted needs. It is said that shamans used to place hot coals in their mouth. They still occasionally pass their hands and arms through fire and pick up hot coals to light tobacco or simply rearrange the fire. The author knew six shamans and a number of their students and never once saw any of them burn herself. They handled fire deftly, as though it was understood that they could burn themselves if they were clumsy, rather than suggesting that they had some special power to protect them from the flames.

The effectiveness of the shamanistic performance is enhanced by a repertory of magical songs or incantations, which are monotonously chanted with only occasional relief from high-wailing stanza endings. They may be classified according to their intended functions as indicated by their meanings. Some of the songs are directed to the Supreme Being, *ñenechen*, others to lesser gods. In the smoke or water-blowing phases of ritual, gods of the north, south, east, and west are alerted to ceremonial needs. There are special songs directed to the shaman's familiar spirits, pillan, who are those of powerful, deceased shamans and some of whom are usually ancestral to the shaman herself. There are songs too designed to lull evil spirits into inaction, to chase evil spirits away, to weaken sorcerer-witches, and so forth. Many of these different kinds of chants may be considered preparatory to the singing of other songs, especially in the sense that they are employed to clear the air or to discharge the build-up of the forces of evil in the immediate ritual precincts before singing trance-inducing songs which, if all goes well, lead to possession of the shaman's body by pillan.

Consequently, songs, their content, specific use, and proper delivery, are a very important element in the mastery of shamanistic lore and techniques. In addition, a shaman must learn to be an almost faultless diagnostician. Her career certainly depends on her success in this area and indeed her life may well depend upon it. Again, songs, chiefly because of their stylized and archaic language, may be of help to the shaman in not only diagnosing illness, but also in divination, in autopsy, in preparing herbal remedies, and in all the other preliminary aspects of curing the sick and/or protecting their closest relatives from contamination by evil spirits.

One of the best informants among the shamans I came to know suggested that she try to "cure" my wife who, after almost eight years of marriage, had not been able to carry a fetus through the whole period of pregnancy. I agreed that she should perform the curing rite on the condition that I be allowed to ask questions before, during, and after the ceremony. It seemed to me on the one hand a splendid way of demonstrating that my wife and I were respectful of Mapuche beliefs, and on the other, an excellent opportunity to investigate the treatment of a common malady (inability to produce offspring) in the kind of detail knowledge that the "case history" of the patient would afford. Although the set of circumstances were, to some degree, staged by the anthropological team, we failed to follow the shaman's advice completely and were reprimanded by her when my wife became pregnant but had a miscarriage.

The details of this episode are interesting. We had known the shaman for more than a month and during that time, visited with her two or three times a week, so on the day of my wife's curing ceremony there was an informal, friendly atmosphere. After clearing up a few preliminary points of information, the curing rite began. My wife stretched out on the earth floor of the shaman's house near the fire. The shaman kneeled next to my wife and began to chant, poke at the fire, prepare the herbs in a shallow wooden tray of water, and have her helper (*thungulmachin*), who, in this case was her husband, prepare her drum by holding it near the heat of the fire to make it taut. All of the preparation took about a half hour.

The shaman began to massage my wife's bare belly, muttering to herself about her condition. Then she started to beat her drum and sing. This went on for approximately forty-five minutes, after which the shaman was apparently in a mild trance state, during which time, she continued to chant. She put down her drum and passed her arms through the fire several times. Her husband threw straw on the fire to make the flames leap in the air. When the flames died down, the shaman lighted a cigarette and blew smoke over my wife in the traditional manner, offering a short prayer to the directions after each puff of smoke. This was followed almost exactly by her spraying water, taken from the herbal tray, over my wife's belly. Then came another massage which, according to the wince on my wife's face, was hard and painful.

Without addressing herself to anyone in the room, the shaman went outdoors to her rewe and offered a prayer to her pillan. This ended the curing ceremony. Before we left her, however, she gave each of us a bottle of water from the herbal tray and told us to drink a little of it morning and night for the next four days.

The medicine was bitter. We poured it on the ground on the fourth day and returned the empty bottles to the shaman, feeling more than a little dishonest. Before the month was out, my wife and I moved away to take up residence on another reservation farther south and did not see the shaman again for many months. In the meantime my wife became pregnant and had a miscarriage. When we finally related this to the shaman she immediately said that we had not followed her directions. Before leaving Chile I was able to see her once again and tell her that my wife was at last carrying a child and had returned to our country. The shaman said that she was happy for us. She also said that her power was so strong that it worked even though we did not follow her advice carefully. She suggested that I make her a gift of a bag of sugar because payment, in these circumstances, always assured success.

In general, if the shaman considers her patient too ill to cure, she will not hesitate to tell his kinsmen that they had delayed too long in seeking her services; perhaps she will even say that her powers are not strong enough to bring about a cure at the advanced stage of the illness. She may well refuse the case. Her decision, of course, depends on her ability to diagnose quickly and accurately. As any diagnostician, the shaman recognizes a range of types of illness to which she attributes various causes. She knows or should know whether or not she is able to work a cure in any given case. A few errors of judgment do not ruin her reputation, necessarily, and only certain cures are felt to endanger her own life by exposing her to the forces of evil. Repeated bungling, however, causes people to lose faith in the shaman's ability and also places her own life in danger frequently. Failures may accumulate to the extent that the community's suspicion is aroused against the shaman. People may whisper about her being aligned with the forces of evil, with being a sorcerer-witch in the guise of a curer.

Some cures are truly dramatic and involve great personal commitment on the part of the shaman, and great faith in the shaman on the part of the clientele. Trepanation, or cutting out a piece of the skull and replacing it, is one of these. To my knowledge, very few of these operations are practiced by Mapuche shamans. However, I knew of three cases of trepanation and became a good friend of one of these patients just after his operation had been performed successfully. He was one of my young informants in the region around the town of Tolten. His name was Secundinas Huenchulaf.[1]

Years before I knew him, Secundinas began suffering severe headaches, the frequency of which increased until he had them several times a week the year round. When I met him, his head was swathed in dirty bandages. At first, he merely said that he had had an operation, and we let it go at that, since he apparently was reluctant to discuss the matter with me.

---

[1] Secundinas means afterbirth in Spanish and was a name bestowed on this young man by his father who did not know the meaning but who liked the sound of the word. Other Mapuche have "odd" names suggested by Chileans (surveyors, soldiers, policemen) who took pleasure in duping the Indians.

As one of my informants, Secundinas used to accompany me on my daily rounds of the reservation on which we lived and, on occasion, to surrounding reservations where he had relatives. On one of our visits to a nearby reservation I stopped in to see a toothless old crone whose reputation hovered between that of a shaman and a sorcerer-witch. Secundinas did the interpreting, but we did not obtain much information from the woman, she being very suspicious of me. Nevertheless, on the basis of the information I received from her and on the strength of some of the stories I had heard about her, I suggested to Secundinas that she was neither shaman nor professional sorcerer. This was just a passing remark which I made to Secundinas on our way home. It triggered the following account of Secundinas' operation and lead, eventually, to an introduction to the shaman who had performed it.

Secundinas suffered from headaches for many months and during that time resorted to almost every kind of treatment he could think of. He took large quantities of the Chilean equivalent of aspirin, to no avail. He stopped drinking *yerba mate* and when that had no effect he began drinking it in excess. When that had no effect he combined aspirin and mate; then he went to a shaman. The shaman gave him one herbal concoction after another for several months. Nothing seemed to help ease the pain or the frequency of the headaches. Finally, the shaman told Secundinas that "the *wekufe* were with him." This is a common expression, which means that one is plagued by the evil spirits and that the case is probably hopeless.

Secundinas had paid the shaman a rather large fee but was still suffering. Furthermore, some of the children on the reservation had begun to call him *wesa lonko* (crazy: possessed by evil spirits). Secundinas was desperate with pain and insult. He went to find a cure from a Chilean doctor in the town of Toltén, again to no avail. He received a cursory inspection from the doctor and a shot of penicillin from the nurse. When he returned to the dispensary a week later he was dismissed without an explanation. He then went to Temuco, a large city with many good doctors, but he fared no better than before. His small amount of money ran out and he was forced to return to the reservation.

Secundinas spent the next few weeks in the house. His father and mother were very sympathetic and did not urge him to work. He became very weak from not eating and from lack of daily exercise. Finally, his father took him to a nearby shaman to seek another cure. The reason Secundinas had not availed himself of this particular shaman's services sooner was that the shaman was a man, and a blind man at that. Mapuche tend to place their trust mainly in female shamans, who are in the overwhelming majority in the reservation area.

This shaman was indeed a strange fellow, and *his* story will be told shortly. He did, however, effect at least a temporary cure for Secundinas. After a brief but intensive diagnostic period lasting only three days, during which time Secundinas slept in the shaman's house and was under his continual surveillance, the shaman prescribed trepanation as the only solution to the problem. He had to cut a hole in Secundinas' head to let out the wekufe. In fact, he cut two "holes," one above each ear, in an operation which lasted for approximately three hours. The shaman used a stainless steel knife (which the author eventually saw) boiled rags to mop up the blood, seagull fat to smear over the wound and keep out the air,[2] and an ordinary needle and strong white thread to sew the scalp back in place. The two "holes" were about the size of a quarter-dollar piece and were very neatly sewn; and in passing my fingers over them I could not detect much bone displacement caused by the trepanning. I urged Secundinas to have his head X-rayed, in order to determine positively if trepanation had actually been done, but he refused to have any more to do with Chilean doctors.[3]

During the few months I knew Secundinas, he had no headaches, was a very alert young man and, apparently, reasonably well adjusted. He performed all phases of farm work besides finding enough time to help the author. Some people still called him "crazy" either to his face or behind his back, but this did not seem to bother him.

By way of concluding this story of Secundinas, I would like to point out that Mapucheland seems to provide a very fruitful field for medical research by doctors who have a greater appreciation for the culture of the Mapuche than local doctors had (1953) when I was in the region. But let us return to a more general consideration of shamanism.

While the shaman's life is exposed to a good deal of risk, it is not by any means over-burdened with considerations of danger, dishonor, and ostracism or expulsion from Mapuche society. Most cures are effected by herbal means, and implemented by magical practices which stop short of spirit possession and the direct grappling with forces of evil. Massage, sucking, and the sleight of hand, which often makes it seem that the shaman has extracted an intrusive object from the patient, do much to relieve the patient's fear of death. Most shamans have picked up a good knowledge of herbs, and the dietary schedule and the herbal infusions prescribed by them are usually sufficient to bring about a real cure. The interpretation of dreams and omens, generally, may be all that a shaman is called upon to do in any given situation. One of the most nagging problems faced by shamans seems to be the treatment of aged people who are ridden with respiratory ailments, heart disease, and other chronic illnesses. Recognizing these symptoms as the harbingers of death, the astute shaman must admit of her inability to counter the "forces of evil" which are responsible.

As with most if not all human relational systems, there is more than one way out of a dilemma. In the shaman's case, the Mapuche people know that there are limits to her power of healing and judge her on a relative scale; that is, it depends on the context and the situation. The culture thus provides certain standardly accepted explanations for her failure in a number of difficult situations.

---

[2] He used the Spanish word *aire*, which has the connotation of evil air or bad air, and sometimes substituted the word *wekufe* in the same context of contamination. A pair of birds, which may well be seagulls, are taken as sacred birds around Toltén.

[3] Although I spoke with Secundinas and the shaman, I am by no means sure that the skull was ever penetrated. The shaman told me that he did cut a hole in the head and, logically (for him, anyway), it was the only way wekufe could have been let out of the head. The scar tissue from the cut was very rough to the touch and hence I was not able to determine if there was actual bone displacement. Although no X-rays were made, I am willing to say that what we refer to technically as trepanation did not in fact occur, despite what the shaman and Secundinas would like us to believe.

August, when there are heavy rains and wide-spread colds and coughing is the Black Month, and during this time the very old and the very young die more frequently than at other times in the year.

Although the shaman has numerous problems in her occupation, the wise shaman cannot only survive them but prosper. If her wisdom is not supplemented by common sense, however, it is not enough to sustain professional shamanistic practice.

Training of the Shaman

To acquire the shaman's knowledge, the neophyte must study with a *bona fide* shaman, often living in the shaman's house, or if not, then making daily visits to each other. Sometimes shamans train their own daughters.

Magical power emanates from the supernatural world and impinges upon a person. It is recognized that would-be shaman's visions tell one of this "power." Dreams, omens, recovery from a serious illness during which one's soul (*am*) has come into contact with the forces of evil and has remained unscathed—all of these things indicate that a person might have power or the potential for acquiring power. If a young woman, for example, has experienced a sense of supernatural power, she may decide for herself, or be encouraged, to undergo training either by her parents, or other relatives, or by a shaman. She may, however, reject the opportunity because of the experience.

Training is costly as well as rigorous. Shamans say that they do not seek out neophytes or accept trainees merely to earn money (or its equivalent in work or gifts of food), although they do not deny that their earnings are thereby enhanced and that their reputation tends to grow if they produce competent shamans.

Let us now look at an interesting, halucinatory experience which decided a sick girl to become a shaman. While by no means all shamans experience the same calling, there is a cultural pattern implicit in the following account, which is an edited quotation recorded in the field.

> When I was a young girl I was very sick and almost died. I had boils all over my body and in my hair. My family was very poor. My mother was a shaman, but she had little success and did not control powerful spirits. Because of this she was unable to cure me. I recovered through my own power and from what I had learned from my mother. I did not have her knowledge, but I had more power.
>
> One day I was tending the sheep when I saw a pure-white lamb walk out of the bushes toward me. The lamb followed me all over. Suddenly, I saw a large kultrun (drum) over the bushes. It was covered with a pure-white lamb skin and there was a blue and white drumstick with bells attached to it. I decided that this vision was presented to me so that I would become a machi. I talked about this with my mother, but she did not know what I should do. She felt that her powers were failing and that she could not instruct me properly. My mother later became a great machi, but now she is too old to practice anymore.
>
> I was sick with boils again, but this time I was able to do my work, I decided to go and get cured by a famous machi who lived in Maquegua, near my natal reservation. Because my father was very poor, his brothers and sisters contributed to the cost of my cure and training. The machi who taught me asked for a lot of money, a new house with room enough for me to sleep alone, and some sheep. I

stayed with her for several years and learned a good deal. I was a good pupil, but she did not teach me everything she knew. After about five years, I was ready. I was almost as good as my teacher, because I had special power that she did not have. I called on my own powerful pillan.

Now I am successful and make a lot of money. It is not easy to be a machi. People think it is easy, and they say that the machi is rich and fat and does not have to work. But my husband works as hard as any man. I work harder than other women. When I am possessed by a spirit, I am close to death. It is dangerous and I do not like to do it. Young machi, as I did myself, like to have the spirits enter them because it is exciting, but I am getting older now and more careful. My house burned down last year, and even the orchard was damaged. I know the evil spirit responsible for this. Long ago I cured a man, but he would not pay me what I asked, and then he died. Now his spirit has been captured by a witch and sent to fight me.

The story of the male machi who did the trepanning should also be of interest. He was one of the most impressive Mapuche I met, and he asked me more questions about my life and where I came from than was asked of him.

I was born blind, and they called me *waillepen* (a strange beast supposed to live in the forest). My mother died because of me. I was raised by my father's sister who lived with us. My father died when I was small, and all my brothers and sisters died. My father's sister married a poor man who came to live in my father's house. He was a bad man. He was just mean. The people chased him away. They called him *kalku* (witch). We went with him to live in a nearby town, where I remained until I was a young man. My step-father had an uncle who lived there who was a machi. We talked together often and I learned very much from him. I had no power then, I did not dream, and I never thought about becoming a shaman. One does not usually think about becoming a machi, one is called to the profession. A machi is similar to a divine being on earth, since the machi talks to the spirits and also talks to the humans. A machi is inbetween.

I used to walk a good deal, and one day I kept on walking. I finally walked as far as Argentina (just over the mountains, not to the coastal cities), and all through Chile (cities included) as far as Puerto Montt. I have crossed the Andes many times. I have heard many things in the houses where I lodged. I worked for people making spoons, baskets, and all sorts of things. I can weave better than a woman, but they have to show me where the colors are.

One night I dreamed that I could see. I had this dream for several months, then I lost it. It bothered me no longer to have this good dream. I finally went back to where I had come from to see my great uncle and found that he had died. I wanted to have him explain things to me. I told another machi about my dream and she liked it. I stayed with her for several years, but never slept with her. She taught me many things.

Gradually, I began to have power. I began dreaming again, and used to dream about my father's uncle, the machi. The woman I was with did not like this; she thought it was dangerous. So I left her. I kept on having dreams, and I began to learn what they meant. I began to work cures on sick people, although I did not know any (herbal) remedies. I made a drum which I beat at night. After this, my dreams were more powerful than ever before. I felt power, and used it to cure sick people where I stayed. I finally came to Pehuelche (near the town of Toltén), where I married a widow with children. Now I have several children by my own semen. My wife has died. I could not save her. Maybe I am losing my power. My daughter (stepdaughter) and her husband live with me and take care of things.

I do not cure anymore. I do not know much about remedies. I only cure very sick people, like the crazy boy who lives near where you and your wife stay. I made two holes in his head to let out the wekufe. I think they are still with him.

He was very crazy and very sick all the time, and the doctor (Chilean) could not help him. He came to me and I cured him in a month, but he is getting sick again. He is crazy. I have no patience with plants and rubbing the body like a *matrona*. Men are more powerful machi than women. They are not afraid to talk to the spirits. I talk with them at night. I frequently have good dreams.

When shamanistic training is completed, the neophyte must demonstrate her ability before a gathering of shamans. Shamans from the same region gather at various times during the year to hold a ceremony for the purpose of revalidating their status as professionals, at which time neophytes may perform before the professional audience. These revalidation rites consist of rounds, the shamans of one region inviting shamans from nearby regions to assist at the celebration and decking out of sacred poles. Invitations are repeated year in and year out on a round basis. At times such as this, the professionals display whatever neophytes they may have in their tutelage whom they consider ready to assume the status of full-fledged shaman.

The Status of Shaman

Once a trainee acquires acceptance by the sisterhood of shamans, she prepares to enter her own practice. This is a time-consuming, difficult, and costly undertaking as well as a risky business. She frequently has to arrange to have a separate house built for herself. From some accounts it seems not uncommon for the new shaman to seek a husband at this time. Since practicing shamans are all of marriageable age, if not actually married. If they are not yet married, they live near and are under the protection of close kinsmen until they marry. Husbands are sometimes trained as shaman's assistants, *thungulmachin*, who interpret trance utterances and perform in a number of important ways for their wives. If the thungulmachin is not the shaman's husband, he is something of a protegee who has to pay for his training. There are interesting variations concerning relatives of the machi, but they cannot be explored here.

Besides training a helper, the shaman must also have a special pole carved, a special drum and drumstick made, and gather, usually at considerable expense, the rest of her equipment. She must also display (advertise) herself to the community for a period of time until they are willing to seek her out for advice. She does this partly by holding small rituals in front of her house, beating her drum and chanting songs well into the night, repeating this performance over several days at a time. She does these things when the spirits are upon her, when she is inspired. The occasions and the quality of the performances indicate to the community whether or not she is a potentially good shaman. Usually in residence among strangers on her husband's reservation, years may pass before she is fully accepted as a curer by the people around her.

Successful shamans are often well-to-do Mapuche. After making difficult cures, and proving to others to be on the side of good, they become respected persons, once their fame has spread. The unsuccessful shamans do not achieve such respect; do not have the proper symbol of office outside their houses, and are regarded as sorcerers rather than curers.

The successful shamans are those who effect the most dramatic "cures" and continue to achieve good results in the day-to-day routine of reservation illness, personal misfortunes, and so forth. They are the ones whose forecasts ("miraculously") come true, whose herbal remedies "work," who lead happy and comfortable lives with husband and children. Although awesome figures to the Mapuche, shamans are not ominous.

Nevertheless, successful shamans do pay a price for their successful and often abundant lives, their well-provisioned larders, and their many sheep and cows. In order to retain fame and fortune, they must continually contend with evil spirits. They must induce their familiar spirits to enter their bodies, meanwhile placing their own souls (*am*) in danger of contamination. Their most dangerous task, and one which is reluctantly assumed and usually avoided, is engaging directly with a *kalku* or witch for the purpose of killing her body. Usually, the shaman will stop with merely (although this, too, is dangerous) identifying, albeit in vague terms, the evil witch whom her client wants discovered. There is more than one kind of ceremony which might result in such identification, and for any one of them the shaman is well paid.

From the client's point of view, his greatest danger lies in losing his soul. If it is not recovered in time by the agency of a shaman, then it is almost certain to be captured by a witch and converted into an evil spirit. The victim, then, either dies or is transformed into a witch's earthly guise. The shaman must grapple with the witch or the witch's evil agent for the soul of the patient. These are costly and prolonged cures, and cure is by no means guaranteed. Success or failure depends mostly on the perspicacity of the shaman in diagnosing illness and deciding whether or not to accept responsibility for a cure. If the shaman refuses to attempt a cure her reputation, as explained above, does not necessarily suffer, even though the sick person dies.

13

Sorcery

B Y MAPUCHE DEFINITION, a *kalku* is a sorcerer-witch who generally is a woman. An embodiment of evil in control of one or more other evil spirits or forces, she performs a black art for a paying clientele but also acts in her own malicious behalf. Anyone may attempt sorcery but, again, by definition, only a kalku will succeed.

In Mapucheland, a sorcerer and a witch are one and the same, and no distinction is made linguistically or behaviorally between them. This is especially interesting because in many African societies that also are patrilineal, ancestor-worshipping, and witch-ridden, sorcerers and witches *are* clearly distinguished. Throughout South America, however, an attempt to make even an analytic distinction would meet with little or no success, and should not be forced. In Mapucheland, the old crone who practices sorcery may turn into a winged head and fly through the night to the witches' cave.

The Sorcerer's Art

I first learned about Mapuche witchcraft by asking about kinship terms and recording genealogies, obtaining both general and detailed descriptive statements about the behavior of the informants' kinsmen. Using key informants, such as chiefs and sublineage elders, complete terminological material was easily gathered. Although using the same informants to learn about reservation-wide genealogical connections proved to be in one sense, unsatisfactory, in another way it was most illuminating. A house-to-house census for mapping the total network of kin relationships, yielded uniform contradictions against certain genealogical information obtained from the key informants. The reason for this was that the informants simply omitted relatives (most often female affines) whom they considered to be witches. Household genealogies included them. Thus, although "every house has its kalku," household members are not disposed to pointing a finger at themselves or their ancestors. Thus, since there are very few selfacknowledged sorcerers, almost all information about sorcery and witchcraft is second-hand.

Witches, like shamans, have "power." Anyone may engage in certain mystical routines—the trappings of sorcery—but real "power," as in the case of shamans, comes in dreams, visions, and so forth, although it may be inherited from ancestors who were kalku and who are disembodied evil forces. One may become a sorcerer-witch through chance misadventure—stumbling upon a witches' cave (*renu*)—or perhaps by contracting a contaminating illness, or having one's soul "captured," and the like. Professional sorcerer-witches train these "converts" in the machinations of the black art.

The mastery of evil is a slow process in Mapucheland. A young woman, for example, who is converted to sorcery requires many years of maturation before emerging (often an elderly woman) as a powerful kalku. As a result, old women bear the brunt of accusations of witchcraft on the reservations and Mapuche crones hobbling about the back alleys of Chilean towns are pointed out as witches who have been driven off their reservations (and some of them have indeed been driven off because of this). Many abuses are heaped on them. Those who remain on the reservations are regarded with suspicion, possibly ostracized, and generally made to feel uncomfortable. They may be judged to have too much land, in the estimation of their coresidents. They are characterized by being, for the most part, inmarried women, widowed, and without the support of grown children. They may have been seen near the scene of some grave misfortune; they mutter to themselves and do "strange" things.

The only self-avowed witch I met in my stay who would discuss the sorcerer's art with me fit the above description perfectly. She lived in a ramshackle house, had a reputation of being hostile toward her neighbors, surrounded herself with jars of magic herbs, wore potent amulets, muttered to herself as she passed people on the road (casting spells?), and did just about everything Mapuche witches are said to do.

Although selfacknowledged witches seem to be few in number, they do exist and they truly believe in their art. Furthermore, they actually believe they unite with fellow witches in caves or in the deep woods. They tell stories about such reunions which, while somewhat vague, are descriptive of the various events. This is certainly not *all* fabrication. If anything, it probably is a dream experience— a true "supernatural" happening.

The witch I knew best told me she had a large clientele, although I was unable to pry from her any names nor, in questioning the neighbors, discover anyone who had used her services. This kind of secrecy was to be expected. She did, however, describe for me some of her exploits. One of these, which she had done many times, is called *koftun*. Koftun is a vengeful act which a female client desires performed against a former lover who has left her pregnant. The sorcerer's contribution, by means of a series of magical acts and incantations, is to render the father of the child sterile thereafter. Given the Mapuche male's desire for children, this would be a terrible penalty.

The story the kalku told is typical of all such tales. She was visited one day by a woman she had never seen before, a women who had come a long distance.

Shaman standing atop her rewe.

Self-acknowledged witch in her house.

The woman had a package with her. She spoke at length with the sorcerer and finally asked her to perform koftun. The kalku immediately asked what was in the package, and was told that it was a dead baby. In this case, the mother had smothered her child; in some cases the mother brings the living child to the sorcerer to be smothered. It seems always to be a male child, since the main feature of koftun consists of removing the testicles of the infant and roasting them slowly over a specially built fire. The notion of contagious magic is inherent in this performance: it is believed that the father's semen will be dried up in the process of roasting his son's testicles.

In the case just mentioned I could not learn anything of the outcome, of whether the sorcerer's performance was successful or a failure. It is possible, of course, for a man in similar circumstances to seek the help of a shaman, who could perform counter magic to combat the sorcerer. Magic works slowly and allows for the victim to attempt to fight it.

I had a detailed account of such a victim near the town of Toltén, although the man was dead before I was able to meet him. He had impregnated a local girl and, when he discovered that she was with child, went to Argentina. The girl went to a kalku and paid for a koftun. I was not able to learn the identity of the girl or the witch. The story I heard, however, told of the man's return from Argentina, because of his fear that koftun had been performed against him. He felt emasculated and returned to his natal reservation to try to discover the kalku through the aid of a shaman. He was unsuccessful in this attempt and began to brood about his condition. Finally, in despair, he went into the swamp near where he lived and ended his life by cutting his throat.

A kalku develops a sense of power, much in the manner of a shaman. She has a dream or a vision of power, feeling that she has inherited this from certain female ancestors who were kalku. Thus armed, she either captures one or more free-wheeling forces of evil, or captures the spirit of an ordinary person, whom she has "contaminated," and uses to her advantage.

Not all Mapuche have the knowledge to answer the anthropologist's questions about shamanism and sorcerery, but there is always some person who is able to give a detailed account of the sorcerer's art and the forces of evil. After a year on the reservations I had the feeling that this was one of the most thoroughly organized segments of Mapuche ideology, and that it was obviously one of the most important things on Mapuche minds.

Dogs, according to the Mapuche, are connected with witches. Observers of Mapuche custom have noted that dogs are chased away from ceremonial fields and from temporary sanctuaries in instances of illness or death. When a kalku "dies" it is said that a dog also dies, the two events being contingent on one another. To complicate this somewhat, it is also claimed that witches never die. What seems to be meant by this is that, although their bodies die (they formerly were dismembered and burned), their evil spirit continues to exist, and, according to Mapuche logic, is taken over by another witch. Dogs are believed to be possessed by witches on certain occasions, and unknown dogs are felt to be temporary embodiments of evil. I was once bayed at by a huge dog, while I was wandering alone in an isolated part of the Island of Chiloe, looking for Huilliche (southern Araucanians). I told of this incident when I returned to Mapucheland and was informed that I had encountered a witch. Retelling the story often after that, all over Mapucheland, it received the same interpretation.

If a Mapuche is confronted by a dog along the path or near someone's house, he does not immediately think of witches. However, if one meets a strange dog and later learns that a death or some other disaster or mishap has occurred in the vicinity, he would surely think that the stray dog had been a witch in disguise.

The Mapuche have a theory about herbs which separates good medicine from bad medicine. Like the ancient Greeks, they believe that internal organs and body juices of certain animals and insects have good or bad qualities. Sorcerers know the array of plants and animals which they may put to their use. Many other Mapuche have similar, if less complete, knowledge of these things. It takes magical power, however, to utilize these plant and animal properties correctly, to extract their "evil essence." Training and practice assist the witch in becoming expert, but evil power determines the degree of her success. A Mapuche is not afraid to pare his nails in his own house provided no strangers are present. He jokes, however, about having his hair cut in town where some witch might obtain the clippings and use them against him. He also might have second thoughts about leaving an extracted tooth in the hands of a Chilean dentist, for Mapuche consider Chileans to be strong witches, especially professionals such as doctors, nurses, and dentists.

When Mapuche cut their own hair, pull their own teeth, and take home remedies, it is not because they are too poor to pay for the service in town or elsewhere. Rather, it is because such things are potentially dangerous and better taken care of in one's own household. Witchcraft is obviously rife in Mapucheland. One takes his chances, propitiates ancestral spirits, carries amulets (women do this more than men), and wears homespun and woven belts which have magical designs (men and women). If these defenses fail, the last resort is to go to a shaman for magical protection.

Like shamans, witches derive additional strength from folklore which gives them a corporate reality, provides them with witches' caves, wings with which to fly through the night, and an everready wardrobe of chimerical and distorted trappings to disguise themselves among humans.

Solidary and Disruptive Aspects of Sorcery

How are the beliefs that "every house has its witch" and "the *wekufe* are always with us" translated into guides for interpersonal and intergroup relationships on the reservations? One way of tackling this question is to phrase it in terms of the kinds of social groupings which are characteristic among the Mapuche. What, for example, is the nature and effect of sorcery among agnates (that is, males of the same lineage), between lineage members and inmarried persons, among sublineages, between dominant and subordinate lineages? Along what lines do the forces of evil run within the reservation community? What forms does sorcery take between reservation communities and what are the lines of cleavage? What is the nature and effect of sorcery between Chileans and Mapuche?

These questions are best phrased in terms of kinship units, residential units, and cultural segments of the frontier zone. They must be boiled down to manageable proportions of size and complexity. They must, of course, direct themselves to the problem of whether sorcery-witchcraft is a unifying or a disruptive aspect of Mapuche life. Is the fabric of Mapuche society held together or strained by concepts of evil and the forms of human behavior they induce?

In addition, there are permissive as well as restrictive forces in operation, which are outside the framework of shamanism and sorcery *per se* but which condition beliefs about sorcery and the alignments of human beings with respect to the forces of evil. There are also different degrees of sorcery practiced in or emanating from different quarters of the social environment.

In the largest possible sense, the Mapuche are pitted supernaturally against all outsiders (*winka*), who are considered potential kalku. Winka fall into two main classes: Chileans and other white persons (mainly foreign missionaries), on the one hand and Mapuche who are unrelated and unknown on the other. In order to define *winka* and to learn more about witchcraft and sorcery, we must begin by defining social and cultural groupings and kinds of evil-doings in relation to these groupings.

The two worlds of the Mapuche and the Chilean are connected by supernatural currents running between them. Chileans rarely use witchcraft to kill the supernaturally stronger Mapuche, but they believe in witchcraft and have their own sorcerers. They regularly use sorcery to try to cheat and dupe the Mapuche who patronize their stores in the towns and along the roadways of the frontier zone, and they must be watched carefully in all matters pertaining to farming and cattle-raising which they engage in with the Mapuche as buyers, sellers, or on a sharecropping basis. All of this is common knowledge among the Mapuche.

Obversely, Chilean peasants and country storekeepers fear Mapuche witches and shamans, classifying both as sorcerers. They believe that animals are spirited away by Mapuche devils who lurk in the night, that crops are ruined by wekufe, whom they equate with the Spanish notion of *duende*. They also know something about the value of certain herbs and the ability of the Mapuche to use them to do harm to Chileans, especially to charm Chilean women and make them pregnant with an Indian child. They know that witranalwe guard Mapuche cattle and houses and make reprisal difficult or impossible. However, they are fully aware that the Mapuche outnumber them in the countryside and are careful not to make open accusations about the evil powers of kalku.

Witchcraft, to which violence, sickness, and death are attributed, is of great explanatory value in the frontier zone, where two different cultures and societies have long been in difficult contact. Evil doings are explained in such a way as to unite local Chileans, on one hand, and Mapuche, on the other, into two camps pitted against one another. The Chilean berates the evil doings of the Indian; the Mapuche rails against the Chilean witches and seeks to make amends to his own neglected ancestral spirits so as to restore the balance of good and evil forces which are abroad in Mapucheland.

Between Mapuche and Chilean, however, homicidal sorcery is not a generally recognized threat, although such "supernatural" killing is believed to have happened. Fear of death is aroused mainly by distant kinsmen, affinal kinsmen of newly incorporated wife-receiving groups or those of former wife-receiving groups with whom marriage ties have broken down and not been renewed. Fear expressed against wife-receiving groups takes two main forms: that of homicidal sorcery, just mentioned, between groups not any longer in sustained marriage relations, and that between two groups (paired as wife-givers and wife-receivers) in sustained relationships in which there is no fear of homicidal sorcery. In the latter case, wife-givers are suspicious of wife-receivers as potential evil-doers who have to be watched closely and made to fulfill sets of important obligations surrounding marriage, birth of children, and care of the dead (that is, care of the inmarried woman and her offspring who die). Wife-givers believe that wife-receiving groups tend to be neglectful of these obligations, that they are envious of the superior social position of the wife-givers, and that they resort to sorcery to undermine this social superiority. This feeling is indicated by the language of fear used in referring to the stereotyped characteristics of *ñillan*, the husband or suitor of a woman of one's lineage, the dangerous one, the potential evil-doer.

The Mapuche do not rationalize the network of fear and obligations systematically. What they do is this: on the occasion of severe illness or death, a person's immediate family suspects that someone outside the reservation community, outside the ritual congregation, but within Mapuche society, has caused the trouble. They place the blame on a formerly marriage-linked group, usually, remembering some former ñillan or other relative connected through a half-forgotten marriage whom they describe as an evil character, untrustworthy, hostile, a potential sorcerer. They think in terms of individuals or households, not in terms of whole lineages, reservations, or marriage categories. But the anthropological model of these marriage categories serves to explain in part how certain kinds of blame are placed, indicating the lines of cleavage which correspond to special kinds of affinal links. Although the Mapuche do not say "We marry our enemies," as has been reported for a number of other societies, their feelings about ñillan and the quality of the marriage bond show that they are concerned about the dangerous possibility of marrying potential enemies (witches).

Short of fears of homicidal sorcery, there is constant fear about less severe forms of sorcery practiced by persons and groups more closely related to one another. An example will suffice. Sorcery is considered a woman's preoccupation, although men also practice it. Thus, women are aligned with the forces of evil and placed on the sinister side of the cosmological universe of the Mapuche. Inmarried women, members of a reservation community by virtue of marriage and patrilocal residence patterns, are notorious for their practice of sorcery against one another. This correlates with the Mapuche saying that every house has its kalku. Within the reservation community, witchcraft is not practiced for homicidal ends but, rather, for the purpose of gaining various kinds of advantage over other persons. Love magic is commonly practiced by women in their own behalf or in behalf of marriageable sons and daughters, to the disadvantage of other women on the reservation. Spells are cast on a neighbor's crops or animals. As I indicated in the Introduction, I was plunged into a situation of this general sort on the first reservation I studied, in which hostile charges and counter-charges of sorcery were made between two families which had at one time shared a common roof.

Fears and charges of sorcery have a clearly disruptive effect on the reservation community when they occur among its own membership. A countervaling force is that the most responsible males on the reservation, elders of the lineage, tend to discount the truth of these charges among the inmarried women. These men, ironically, are the very ones who fulfill the obligations to ancestral spirits, who organize the ceremonial life of the reservation. They are responsible for maintaining a favorable supernatural balance in the universe, and this common responsibility helps unite them against the forces of evil.

14

Death and Burial Rites

RITES SURROUNDING DEATH and agricultural fertility, and the ideological framework they symbolize, are together the greatest integrative force at work among the Mapuche. Although this chapter is devoted to a discussion of death and burial rites, consideration is also given to the entire ritual congregation which is involved in agricultural fertility rites as well.

My wife and I were discouraged from attending the first wake and burial service, which took place near the reservation on which we first lived. During the first agricultural fertility ceremony that we attended we were actually driven away by a drunken man on horseback whose painted face made him appear more menacing than he really was. He was chief and ritual leader of his reservation, and months later explained to me, after I gained his confidence, that protocol forced him to ban me from the first day's rituals of the *ñillatun* ceremony. Pointing out that this seemed to contradict my experience in other parts of Mapucheland and wondering why, at that very moment, I was allowed in his own postharvest ceremony, he replied that I had looked so foreign at the time of the first ceremony that the people did not trust me. Now, after more than four months in Mapucheland, my ankle-length poncho (which I carried with me to use as a blanket in the fall of the year), my floppy felt hat, my boots, and, probably, my general manner, served to make me less foreign. The original conspicuousness, it is now apparent, heightened the peoples' distrust and fear, and made it very difficult for me to obtain information about births, marriages, and deaths during my first few months' residence.

The Rationale

The concept central in importance to Mapuche religious morality is that of a sustained and responsible link between the living and the dead. The living are responsible for the propitiation of the dead. Ritual is designed to maintain

ancestral spirits in an otiose condition. Through adequate expiatory and supplicatory rites, they are contained in a halcyon afterworld which is not contaminated
by evil spirits. Neglect of these spirits or imperfection of ritual initiates action
on their part; they return to Mapucheland to advise their descendants of their
neglectful behavior, during which time the spirits are subject to capture by witches
and, possibly becoming contaminated and converted into them in the process.
Spirits can also return in visions and dreams to assist their descendants in many
important matters of reservation life. On these occasions they are, likewise, in
danger of capture by the forces of evil. In fact, when one does not dream of
ancestors for many years he becomes uneasy and fears that they may have been
turned into witches or other evil spirits (*wekufe*).

The spirits of ancestral chiefs (*lonko*) however, are felt not to be endan-
gered by the forces of evil. This indicates that they are on the order of the divine
beings themselves—that is, not susceptible to contamination by kalku. The evil
forces, however, can and do thwart the benevolent intentions of departed chiefs
(sons of the gods) and even the lesser deities, when the balance tips in favor of
them. Thus, when there is some ritual inadequacy, the work-a-day world of the
community is disrupted. In this sense, imperfection is the equivalent of sin.

The weight of good over evil is maintained or reinstated generally through
mass propitiation of ancestors and deities in the ñillatun and funeral ceremonies.
In these two ceremonies the most pressing matters are dealt with: the eternal
struggle between good and evil.

How are these expiatory and supplicatory rituals arranged? What is the
nature of the ancestral group, of the pantheon of gods, of the assemblage of
Mapuche who participate in these ceremonies? It is not enough to say that the
Mapuche propitiate their ancestors and the gods. This is only the beginning of
the investigation. We can be much more precise and discuss the physical and
supernatural aspects of ritual in a manner detailed enough to shed light on problems of cultural and social constancy and change. We must focus attention on
the kinds of ancestors involved on specific ritual occasions, on the kinds of deities,
their rank, their regional significance, and on ethnic and genealogical ties between
the living and the dead. From specific cases, emerge the general Mapuche notions
of good and evil, inferiority and superiority, and similar complementary concepts.

The Assemblage

A death takes place on a reservation. In a few hours word spreads. Perhaps
the death was anticipated by neighbors, and if so, they know about it almost
instantly. They have probably spoken of the sick person to other neighbors, to
relatives on other reservations, and so on. Thus, word of the death will spread
very rapidly from one reservation to the next.

One day Alonqueo and I had set out in the morning to have a bag of wheat
milled on a nearby Chilean farm (*fundo*). We passed several Mapuche along the
road and Alonqueo had a few words to say to each of them. I was able to catch
the words "death," "wake," and "burial," and asked Alonqueo who had died. He

said that he would take me to the wake that evening and that we would have to hurry to the flour mill and back so that we could make preparations. At my urging, we attended the wake two nights in a row, so that I could form a better opinion of how it was conducted and, mainly, of what kinds of relatives and friends attended. Each night there was an almost complete change in the group of mourners and Alonqueo and others told me that this was always the way. At the funeral ceremony, after the period of wake, all these groups plus many others gather together once again for the final rites. Just who are these mourners?

The assemblage at any funeral rite (*awn*) is made up of specific kinds, orders, or degrees of the mundane as well as the supernatural *interesados* (interested persons and spirits). This is also true at any agricultural fertility ceremony. The deceased at the wake and funeral and the sacrificial animals and plants at the fertility rite dramatize and make especially poignant the link between the world of the living and the dead. The people who participate in, or merely attend as spectators, either of these ceremonies demonstrate their pureness of heart (*kumepiuke*) with respect to both the living and dead as well as to the deities.

In bare outline, the assemblage may be described as follows: there is the supernatural component made up of lineal ancestors (mainly males of social prominence); the mythical ancestors, who are potentially on their way to becoming regional deities; the lesser gods, such as the god and goddess of the southwind, god and goddess of thunder, god and goddess of the sea, and so forth; and the Supreme Being, *ñenechen*, who is usually considered to preside over all matters of life and death. Especially at funerals, the spirits of ancestors of the recently deceased are of great importance, giving a lineal cast to the ceremonial activities.

The human sector consists of the several patrilineal descent groups most responsible (that is, those in closest relationship to the deceased by ties of blood or marriage) to look after the well-being of the dead person's spirit; the wives (inmarried women) of the male core of these descent groups; and representative guests within the regionally defined ritual congregation. Sometimes important persons outside the ritual congregation are included, especially in the event of the death of an important chief or shaman. The emphasis which is placed on certain lineages and residential kingroups, as well as on ancestors (or the more important gods), depends on the nature of the ritual, whether it is a funeral or a fertility ceremony.

Let us consider first the general and customary composition of the funeral assemblage, using as our reference a deceased spouse (male or female) who has lived under conditions of matrilateral marriage and patrilocal residence. Regardless of whether the ceremony is in behalf of the man or his wife, the major responsibility for the conduct of the funeral service rests with the patrilineal kinsmen of the man, kinsman who are in residence with their inmarried women on the man's natal reservation.[1]

Next in importance is the patrilineal descent group of the woman (wife). If it is the woman who has died, her surviving spouse's lineage is obliged to care

---

[1] This specific, albeit somewhat awkward, phrasing is in the interest of clarity. It might be considered esthetically more pleasing to write merely that a man's kinsmen are responsible for the care of himself or his wife; but this would be too vague a description.

properly for her wake and burial. If it is the husband who has died, the lineage of his widow must assume the responsibility of ritual assistance of his funeral, on his reservation.

In all cases, the wife's patrilineal kinsmen are the most *highly honored guests* at the funeral ceremony, reflecting their superiority to the husband's lineage as wife-givers in the system of matrilateral alliance.

There are other persons whose attendance is considered as obligatory, because of their affinal ties to the husband's lineage. These are lineages into which women of his own patrilineage have married. If these lineages do not send representatives, they may be suspected of harboring persons who have brought about the death of either the man or woman whose funeral is being conducted. On occasions when these wife-receiving affines are neglectful of their moral obligations, suspicion is aroused and they may even be accused of homicidal sorcery.

Funeral ceremonies are not wholly lineage affairs however. Nonrelated coresidents of the reservations involved are also expected to attend the services or send representatives. They constitute an important segment of the participants and lend the affair a parochial aspect—and also, by their attendance, clear themselves of suspicion of homicidal sorcery. Otherwise, funeral ceremonies are organized largely on a genealogical basis.

Funeral Services

When a person dies he (or she) is laid out on a bier in his house. First, however, he is thoroughly washed and dressed in his best clothes (European dress for men and Mapuche dress for women) by his closest kinsmen. He usually remains in this state for the ritually perfect four days, during which time relatives and friends attend his wake (*kurikawin*: black gathering; *moñetun*: curing or sustaining ceremony), and ready themselves for the imminent burial services.

The dead person is placed in a coffin as soon after death as possible. The coffin may be one of the old type, constructed by the family of the deceased (elder) in anticipation of his death and under his supervision, or it may be one of the newer and less expensive pine boxes which are sold in most Chilean towns. The old-fashioned coffin is made out of a split and hollowed tree trunk. It takes not only much time and labor to make, but requires one (at least for those Mapuche living in treeless areas) to make a trip to a well-forested zone where there are stands of old virgin timber, in order to cut a proper tree. Then, the trunk must be hauled, usually in a laborious fashion by ox-cart (helpers riding in the cart and the tree dragged behind) over as much as fifty miles. Not anyone is able to carve the coffin, so it is usually necessary to hire an expert axman to do the job. With the charring, which is needed to soften the wood, as much as two months may be required to prepare the traditional coffin. If the craftsman is paid the specialist's price for day labor, which varies from region to region, the job could amount to a sizeable cost to the family involved.

If the deceased further requires that his body be smoked, even in a token manner (in other words, merely ritually rather than with the idea that it would be preserved), the cost of the funeral increases. If the deceased commands that his body be eviscerated, drained of body fluids, and so forth, in addition to the former requirements, then the costs are beyond the reach of the vast majority of Mapuche families. It stands to reason, therefore, that chiefs and important shamans are the only ones who can be assured of such burial. Most Mapuche coffins are pine boxes bought in town and painted black.

Although the coffin may have been homemade or bought in anticipation of the death, in most cases it is purchased in town immediately after death. The Mapuche maintain that they adhere to the spirit of the law (*admapu*) by having the box painted black—although the tree trunk is never painted black, as far as I know—and, thus, dissociate themselves from Chileans who, of course, make or purchase pine boxes.

The Mapuche coffin is placed on a bier off the ground. It must remain off the ground until the time of interment, at which stage of the funeral matters are completely reversed and the container of the body is placed beneath the ground, while the spirit is supposed to soar. The corpse is displayed for four days, if it is possible to adhere to this ideal number of days. This is a very deliberate manner of handling the corpse, one which postpones interment until a propitious time. It enables the mourners to drive away the evil spirits from the house and its environs by a process of encirclement, a ceremony called *amulpellun*, which is also, of course, designed to hasten the safe departure of the deceased's spirit. The danger of the dead person's spirit becoming contaminated by the forces of evil is very great, and the corpse itself is considered to be dangerous and potentially contaminating to the observers at the wake. If all goes well, this danger is greatly reduced by the mourning procedures conducted during the four preceding days of the kurikawin or monetun. The wake ends the first phase of the burial ceremony.

All spirits of pure Mapuche are felt by the mourners to linger in or near the house in which the wake takes place, before departing for the afterworld—a place considered to be very far away from Mapucheland. Whether or not the trip to the afterworld is successfully accomplished depends on the mourners; that is, provided their propitiation ceremonies have greater power than the machinations of the wekufe. If the ceremony of wake and burial fails, the spirit falls into the hands of the forces of evil, the embodiment of which is the kalku or sorcerer-witch. If the funeral service is successful, contamination is avoided and the spirit departs for *nomelafken*, where, ideally, it enjoys an undisturbed life-after-death with kinsmen.

During the four days of wake there is a procession of visitors. On the first day arrive those of the same and surrounding reservations, neighbors as well as kinsfolk. Nowadays, during most of the year, Mapuche are able to travel easily up and down the frontier zone without much delay, although the truck, bus, and train fare involved is usually considered very expensive. Despite expenses, relatives from afar usually arrive within the four day period of wake and are, therefore, on hand for the single day of primary and secondary burial.

After the four days of wake, the coffin is placed on a bier in the center of a field, which is a distance from the deceased's house (and usually on fallow farm land) and where the funeral assemblage is able to congregate in order to pay its respects (proper, traditional, and with an eye to their own well-being) to the dead.

Once the body has been removed from the house to the ceremonial field, it is possible to make an analytical separation between "burial" and "wake," a distinction signalized by formal orations from lineage elders or other well-informed Mapuche, called *weupin*. Weupin signifies a dialogue between the living and the dead, a link between mortal men and their ancestral chiefs and other forebears.

This kind of eulogy, known as weupin, involves the praises of the dead. This oration seemed to an outsider, as being of major significance to an understanding of Mapuche culture and social institutions. The spectators, even though half-drunk with wine and chicha, were very attentive to the weupin orations. I had the feeling that there was, especially on this occasion, an abundance of *kumepiuke*, or goodness or pureness of heart, which is a word spoken frequently by visitor and host during the formalities of the mourning assemblage.

Relatives of several kinds, as well as any friends of the deceased (rarely a friend if not a relative of some sort), and friends and relatives of the deceased's kinsman, begin to assemble on the ceremonial field, within view of the bier and coffin, on the morning of the fourth day after death. A sumptuous meal is prepared for the assemblage by the household members of the dead person, with many contributions of food and labor from the closest patrilineal kinsman of the deceased— and at great cost to those who contribute.

This performance, accompanied by numerous weupin orations, marks the end of the wake and initiates the ceremony which is concerned with the final disposal of the dead. Although the spirit of the dead person is still lingering about the ceremonial field at this time it is believed that there is now much less risk of its being captured by the forces of evil.

I have witnessed funerals at which more than 1,000 adults were in attendance. On such occasions etiquette does not encourage condolences, and they are never given during the period between the wake and the time the coffin is interred in the cemetery, although they are readily offered during the wake and after burial. The display of the corpse in the field and the weupin orations about the dead person and his living relatives and ancestors together constitute a most decorous program of respect not only to the dead, but also to his direct-line ancestors and to his closest agnates and affines. At least at the beginning of this transitional day, the assemblage remains quite solemn. Let us take a closer look at this phase of the funeral ceremony.

Early in the morning, the participants begin to arrive. The men line up on horseback along part of the ceremonial field. If the assemblage is very large, the riders completely encircle the field or make a semicircle around it, about 100 yards from the bier. They wait there, in stiff position, until they are greeted by their host, a patrilineal kinsman of the dead man or an affinal of his wife. On this solemn meeting, kinship terms are exchanged between the host and the horsemen, and even nonrelatives are addressed by kinship terms. These are generational terms, such as uncle, father, brother, and so forth.

The women and children usually walk to the funeral or come in the family ox-carts, especially if they are close relatives of the deceased or his family. Bringing with them ample quantities of bread or other food to make the ceremony more impressive, they remain apart from the men throughout most of the day. Their gathering, largely because of the presence of the children (including suckling infants) is much less solemn than that of their husbands and grown sons. Later, however, it is the women who wail and tear their hair and clothing, while the men remain much more composed.

An abundance of food and wine is supplied by the immediate family of the dead person and much more is contributed by guests, especially members of the host group (that is, members of the same lineage as the man as well as by members of the subordinate lineages of his reservation, who might be especially suspect in the case of the death of his wife).

A transformation takes place as the wine begins to flow. Approaching drunkenness, the men and women begin to mingle and a note of confusion enters the funeral scene, which was so orderly and composed at the outset. However, after the anthropologist has had an opportunity to know these people, what appears at first to be complete confusion, ending in drunken stupor, accidents, even serious bodily injury and another death, is really only part of the release due the living, without which the traditional exhortation of evil spirits could not occur.

During the time the coffin is open and on display in the field—from after sunrise until early afternoon—the gathering views the corpse close by. Some viewers weep naturally, it seems, while others shed almost professional mourners' tears. Alonqueo confirmed my first impressions, adding, that these weepy mourners, because they were not patrilineal kin of the dead man, were expected to cry the most.

Close relatives and friends deposit coins, articles of clothing, personal trinkets, and so forth, in the coffin before it is closed. All of this, including the public and personal prayers, is designed to speed the spirit safely to the afterworld.

As the name of this phase of the funeral ceremony (*weupin*) suggests, it is a time for orations and eulogies spoken over the bier of the deceased. Any serious and formal remark, exclusive of short magical incantations made by those who pass by the coffin (mostly women), is considered *weupin*. Most speeches are short. Some, however, are long and last for about an hour. These are delivered by elders of the lineage, who are familiar with genealogies and best able to link the deceased with branch lines of his own lineage as well as with those affinal connections which the people would consider most important, with respect to impressive kinship links to the dead person and ancestral spirits which have general importance to the reservation community and the congregation as a whole.

Persons who speak what is recognized as formal weupin are almost always males. They are elders of the patrilineage of the deceased (man), his widow, and elders of other lineages connected by marriage bonds with that of the deceased.

The virtues of the dead person are praised and explained in a genealogical framework. These orations, while continuing through the late morning and early afternoon, tend to be concentrated at the beginning of this phase of the funeral (as introductory remarks) or at the end (as a summation). A point of major interest here is that in formulating genealogical connections to important ancestors, the orators, sometimes with full awareness but sometimes inadvertently, manipulate the genealogy of the deceased. They tinker with the genealogical position of some ancestors which affects the total framework of relationships. For instance, an ancestor called Wenchulaf Kurikeo during the genealogical reconstruction of the weupin, turns out to be, upon the anthropologist's own genealogical detective work, two ancestors lumped into one and dressed up in the splendid attributes of each. If, and this is not the only possibility, Wenchulaf is a direct line ancestor of one branch of a lineage and Kurikeo of another, then lumping their attributes into one ancestral figure draws branch lines together and makes for closer degrees of relationship among the living members of the lineage. According to Mapuche values, this serves as a solidarity measure—especially at the crisis time of death— integrating the survivors with the dead person's lineage mates. The kinship termi- nology, being of the "classificatory" kind, facilitates this sort of manipulation by its very vagueness. And this manipulation of genealogies, being heard for the first time by most of the assemblage, who evaluate it in terms of their individual knowledge and interest, believe it and pass it along as truth to others (the anthro- pologist included). Thus, funeral rites are, in effect, classrooms where Mapuche elders impart detailed comments on Mapuche values in reference to ancestral spirits and in a genealogical framework; they are also historical events during which local history is retold and, significantly, slightly refashioned.

Once the orations are finished, the coffin is transferred to the cemetery by pallbearers (or in an ox-cart), and placed in the grave. Usually, libations are poured over the grave as it is being filled in, and more wine is drunk by the few closest kinsmen who accompany the deceased. Most of the mourners remain on the ceremonial field on which the corpse had been displayed. Those who are able (and not stupified by drink) begin to leave for their homes shortly after the interment party has returned from the cemetery.

If the funeral ceremony has been successful, its three main objectives have been accomplished. The remains of the dead have been disposed of in a ritually perfect manner; the spirit has made a proper departure for the afterworld; the living have discharged their obligation of mourning. Then begins their life- long responsibility of propitiating this particular ancestral spirit along with all other "hawks of the sun."

15

Fertility Rites

A S WE HAVE SEEN, there is both a spiritual and a worldly connection between the Mapuche funeral and agricultural fertility ceremonies. One is similar and complementary to the other, insofar as their concepts relate to ancestral spirits, purification, and sacrifice, and affect the behavior of the ritual congregation in similar ways.

These ceremonies are described now and again in the literature on the Mapuche. Without fail, however, they are described as separate rites and, although they are certainly distinguishable, no author has, to my knowledge, made the point that they are also inextricably bound together by the Mapuche concern with ancestors' spirits and purification.

I was not aware of the connection between the ceremonies until an informant became somewhat annoyed with me for not understanding what he was describing while he was talking to a couple of other Mapuche. He was talking to them about *awn*, but the description was rather different from any funeral I had heard about. I had not been invited to a funeral yet, nor had I witnessed a fertility ceremony. The man was speaking mixed Araucanian and Spanish and I had great difficulty following him.

Sensing his annoyance, I wanted to show him that I did understand something of what he was saying and asked, "Whose funeral are you talking about?" The three men looked at me and the speaker explained in very slowly articulated Spanish—which was meant to be insulting to the ignorant stranger—that *awn* did not only mean funeral, it also meant *ñillatun* (fertility rite), part of which was felt to duplicate the main feature of the funeral rite: purification of the ceremonial field so that ancestors would not suffer contamination from the forces of evil. Once this connection is seen, the importance of ancestral propitiation among the Mapuche takes on new meaning. Proper care of ancestors' spirits is a step in propitiating the aggregate of gods and, as noted, is central to the Mapuche value system and the ideas which constitute Mapuche morality and permeate every facet of their social activities.

Agricultural Fertility Rites

There are clear indications in Mapuche ethnographic literature that ñillatun ceremonies, which are today essentially agricultural fertility ceremonies, were once geared to other Mapuche interests and basic needs. Elements have been dropped from the ceremony—military concerns, completely—and others added, or, as in the case of agriculture and cattle raising, given greater emphasis. The resulting ceremony and its ideological base, which is essentially uniform throughout Mapucheland, is nowadays a composite of centuries of adaptive reintegration.

In the ñillatun rites the Mapuche congregate to state their needs to their ancestors and their gods. The emphasis is on agricultural needs, but in time of general sickness or general disaster from earthquake, the latter concerns are given prominence. The ceremony is, therefore, flexible and, presumably, has always been so. Prayers are offered to the Supreme Being, ñenechen, to the lesser or regional gods, to ancestral spirits, and generally designed to secure the well-being of the supplicants. The Mapuche pray for many things: health, the conquest of good over evil, agricultural success, an abundance of crops and animals, good weather, kinds of crops, and so forth. Except for the total lack of concern with military matters, it is likely that the same prayer format exists today as it did since the Spaniards first recorded Mapuche religious beliefs centuries ago. Emphasis, however, has been geared to agricultural needs in an area of diminishing crop yields and increasing population pressure, brought about by the reservation system.

Agricultural fertility ceremonies are usually held in the pre- and post-harvest seasons. There is no exact ritual calendar, although the rituals are performed in the seasons indicated and usually around the full of the moon, at which time the fertility-bestowing god and goddess of the moon (kuyenfucha/kushe) are considered to be most receptive to human prayer and sacrificial offerings. The ceremonies are planned by chiefs, who are ideally ñillatufe or ritual priests, and elders, who are heads of sublineages on the reservations. There is a highly systematic arrangement for the holding of ceremonies which involves the obligatory participation of the chiefs and members of several reservations in a cyclical pattern of responsibility. We will take a closer look at this patterning of responsibility after describing the ñillatun ceremony itself.

Several reservations usually combine their efforts in an agricultural fertility ceremony, especially in the ceremony which takes place after the harvest and which is given in thanks for the harvest. The Mapuche know in general when these rituals will be held. The chiefs of several reservations get together to make arrangements. Notice of the exact date (using the Chilean calendar) is passed by the chief of each reservation involved in the performance to his neighbors. Word is passed around in the form of a statement of the exact purpose of the ceremony, what contributions of food and animals are expected of each participant, and so on.

Preparation for the ñillatun ceremony has two main aspects, the formal preparation engaged in by the leaders of the ceremony, and the personal preparation engaged in by the individuals who participate in ñillatun. Individual families make elaborate preparations. They ready their clothing, patching it or buying cloth and making new clothes; they repair their ox-carts and grease the wheels; they shine their silver, heirloom jewelry; they curry their horses and oxen, clipping tails, fattening the animals, and so on. They usually have about a month's notice before the ceremony is staged.

The formal preparation is handled by the ñillatufe and his assistants, the other chiefs and elders. They visit the ceremonial field on the host reservation. Each reservation, ideally, has its ceremonial field; if not, that of an adjacent reservation is used. The ceremonial field is tidied up by the elders and helpers of the host reservation, and the main and secondary altars prepared, as well as the *ramadas* or cubicle-like shelters of boughs to be used by participants during the ceremony.

The main altar is either an old carved effigy post or simply a crotched tree trunk of recent origin. It is surrounded by boughs of trees which are considered sacred (cinnamon, apple, *maqui*) and which are renewed each year the ceremony is held. Now the field is ready for the ritual. The officials offer prayers to their ancestors and to ñenechen, the Supreme Being. A small sacrificial fire is made.

On the day of the general ceremony, the participants and invited guests (spectators) begin to arrive. The ñillatufe and his assistants are on the scene much earlier than the first ordinary participants. They devote their time to final preparations, which include the propitiation in turn of the ancestors of each lineage represented at the ñillatun. At the time of this propitiation, which I was never allowed to witness because of its highly sacred character, the ñillatun and funeral ceremonies are almost indistinguishable. The chiefs and sublineage elders recount their genealogies and ask their ancestors for a blessing on the ceremony. They chase the evil spirits away from the ceremonial field. They attend to the main altar (*rewe*) but they focus their attention on the secondary altar, the *llangi*, which is the symbolic equivalent of the bier at the funeral ceremony.

When the sun is at about 9 o'clock, the participants and guests begin to flock onto the ceremonial field. Some of them occupy ramadas already set aside for them, others hastily construct windbreaks, others merely seat themselves next to their horses or ox-carts which, after everyone is settled, form a ring or a semicircle around the ceremonial field. By this time the officials have staked out the sacrificial sheep or oxen, gathered wood for the special ceremonial fires (at the main and secondary altars), and have placed wooden bowls of sacrificial grains and libational offerings at the main altar.

This first day of the customarily two-day ceremony is considered extremely sacred. No alcoholic drinks are permitted, although a few of the spectators always seem to disregard the law. If they become disorderly, they are evicted from the ceremonial field by officials called sergeants, who have staffs of office with which they are allowed to club offenders.

The second day of the ceremony draws many spectators, as distinguished from responsible participants, and is characterized by a good deal of visiting, gossiping, and often the drinking of wine or hard cider. A number of profane items and actions are then introduced to the ceremony.

The ñillatun rites themselves are divided into four main parts on both days of the ceremony, each part and each day largely duplicating the other. Ideally, they should be identical, but variations do occur.

The four main parts of each day of the ceremony may be separated into the early-morning, the mid-morning, the early-afternoon, and the late-afternoon sections. These should be conducted unerringly by the ñillatufe, the chief-priest, who has the assistance of other ñillatufe, chiefs from participating reservations, and other ritual specialists. Sometimes shamans are invited to participate, since they may fill a gap in knowledge about religious lore. Officials called captains and sergeants are present to help preserve order, curtailing drunkenness and preventing fights and any other disturbances which would pollute the ritual atmosphere and limit the effectiveness of the ceremony.

The captains and sergeants are selected by the chiefs (ñillatufe) of the several reservations in participation. They are usually heads of sublineages of their chief's lineage or are heads of subordinate lineages on their reservation. Most of these officials cannot aspire to assume the role of ñillatufe, given the nature of the Mapuche system of patrilineal succession, in which a chief's eldest son customarily succeeds to his father's position as chief—political leader, economic leader (titular), religious leader—by virtue of mainline kinship. But these subordinate leaders are brought into ritual (and other) responsibility through a time-honored social division of labor which hinges on the system of localized patrilineal descent groups, bounded by reservation lines, and a product of traditional values and the superimposed reservation system of the Chilean government.

The ñillatufe offers an opening prayer to ñenechen and ancestral spirits. This is done in an archaic language that most of the participants do not fully understand.[1] The priest stands near the main altar with his assistant priests to his right. The ñillatufe, upon finishing the prayer, commands his captains and sergeants to have the male participants commence the encirclement of the ceremonial field (awn). As mentioned, the encirclement, as in the funeral ceremony, is to clear the field of evil spirits who might otherwise contaminate the ancestral spirits present. The men who perform the awn are mounted on their finest horses and dressed in their finest clothes (usually of the Chilean huaso type), some of them wearing sheepskin masks, or painted faces, to hide their identity from the evil gods.

The awn or encirclement describes the ceremonial field. Sometimes the ceremonial field on a reservation is in the midst of farmland. When it is, it is frequently squared, indicating a place which should neither be plowed nor grazed. The manner of Mapuche plowing results in the square shape of the ceremonial field. This visible fact contradicts, however, the Mapuche statement that their ñillatun field is circular. The circularity, which has great symbolic value for the Mapuche, is actually seen only in the performance of awn and the disposition of participants around the ceremonial field. The awn riders make a circle around the two altars, encompassing both of them. So tight is the riding circle of the horsemen and so great their speed, the horses are actually leaning inward as they gallop counterclockwise around the sacred ground. The Mapuche have a reputation as good horsemen and the awn is the time of their greatest performance.

Living the day-to-day life among the Mapuche, one realizes that they are different from Chilean peasants, but the characteristic beliefs and social organization

---

[1] I recorded these prayers phonetically. Then I read them to the ñillatufe. He always told me that such-and-such words were no longer known by the people, sometimes he did not know their meaning himself. The very unintelligibility of the prayers was considered sacred.

of the Mapuche do not usually make the differences vibrant. But in watching the encirclement at the ñillatun ceremony one sees "Indians." Mapuche horsemen, who plod along the ox-paths every day, are now galloping around a pagan altar. The spectators are almost hypnotized with interest. The riders, many of them bared to the waist, masked or painted, shout, in a manner reminiscent of Hollywood Indians, *Ay! Ay! Ay! Ay!* The dust flies and mingles with the pungent cooking fires which are already cooking the midmorning meal. There are galloping horsemen, a thousand or more Mapuche crowded together to witness the encirclement, a haze of smoke and dust, a thundering of horses' hooves in the stillness, a pile of wheat chaff and a thatched house or two in the near distance, the snow-capped volcano hovering on the horizon. It is an impressive sight.

The awn envelopes the ceremonial field. The riders encircle the two altars. The main altar is called the *rewe*, as is the shaman's "sacred pole," which is what the word means; the secondary altar, as mentioned, is called the *llangi*, a bier, as in the wake and funeral ceremony, and stands about 100 yards from the main altar, in an easterly direction (the orientation of Mapuche ceremonies is toward the east).

The riders race around the perimeter of the field and from time to time raise cries to chase away the evil spirits. This act, as has been indicated, is essentially a duplication of the *amulpellun* ceremony which involves the encirclement of a dead person's house at the time of the wake. The horsemen are most impressive and hold the full attention of the audience. They ride in a column of two's, led by standard bearers and their rear brought up by a sergeant carrying a long staff of office. Taking their cues from the captain and/or the ñillatufe, they dismount near the secondary altar where they tether their horses and begin a short foot-dance around the llangi before returning to the main altar. When they come to the main altar they participate in the purun (dance) which has started there.

The purun is a slow dance, again of encirclement, which takes place around the main altar and lasts for roughly fifteen minutes. The ñillatufe gives commands to the captains and sergeants to step up or decrease the dancing tempo. Both men and women dance in the purun, in a counterclockwise encirclement of the rewe (main altar). They wear sprigs of the sacred branches of cinnamon, apple, and *maqui*, which decorate the altar. They may also carry kernels of maize, wheat, and other domestic plants.

Music is provided by a number of players who know the traditional instruments, such as the whistles (*pifulka*), which are made of stone, pottery, or wood; the trumpets (*trutruka*), made of Chilean bamboo covered with leather and tipped by a cow's horn; and drums (*kultrun*), made of shallow wooden "bowls" covered by sheepskin or, sometimes, calfskin. All are native instruments, described in the earliest chronical reports more than 400 years ago, and all are homemade.

After the ñillatufe gives the command to end the purun, he orders the dancers to line up in a special manner. He lines up a row of men and a row of women. Each row extends east (toward the secondary altar) from the main altar. Now the men face the women, and the ñillatufe begins his second major prayer of the morning. During the intervals between stanzas of this prayer, the opposing lines of men and women are commanded to do in-place dancing. The dance ends after ten minutes or so, when the dancers, especially the older ones, are panting and perspiring heavily.

In-place dancing during ñillatun ceremony.

At this juncture, the ñillatufe, with the assistance of his captains and sergeants, as well as other officials, kills one of the sacrificial sheep, which has been staked near the main altar. This is a bloody episode in the ceremony, which is enacted at least once more during the ritual, and, if the ritual is traditionally perfect (from the participants' views and from the anthropologists' who have scanned the literature), the sacrifice will be made in the morning and afternoon of the first and second day. In this manner, four sheep are given to the ancestors and the gods.

The details of the performance are of especial theoretical interest, aside from their intrinsic appeal. The ñillatufe, bleeding the sheep to death, cuts off its right ear. Holding it above him in his right hand, he then offers a prayer to the gods. The priest-chief then places the sheep's ear on the main altar, in the crotch (or on top of the head of the effigy pole) and prepares to open the chest cavity of the sheep. The sheep's heart is removed. The ñillatufe holds it in his right hand over his head and offers another prayer. Then he bites into the heart, which is still palpitating or twitching, and passes it onto the next chief in line to his right. The next person also bites into the sheep's heart and passes it on to the next official until the end of the line is reached. The priest-chief then receives the heart from the last official who has held it and places it in the crotch of the *rewe*.

A bowl of sheep's blood is then placed at the right side of the altar, from which the ñillatufe occasionally sprinkles the ritual fire (*llupe*) near at hand. Some of this blood is also burned on the fire near the secondary altar. After this is done, in-place dancing is again performed by the two lines of men and women.

A few officials are designated to take the carcass of the slaughtered sheep to the llangi fire at the secondary altar. They skin and quarter the animal. The skin is brought back to the main altar and placed on the ground near it. Some or all of the sheep is cooked on the llangi fire. The smoke which rises from the burning sheep is considered a special tribute to ancestral spirits, that arising from the fire near the main altar is considered to be especially propitious to ñenechen and the pantheon. The overlap between funerals and fertility rites is thus symbolized with magnificent clarity in the ñillatun ceremony. In this instance the observer is able to see the ideological and behavioral connection based on the Mapuche notion of the relationship between man and the supernatural.

After the first sheep is sacrificed, the ritual priest begins the second part of the early morning prayer. This time concern is (or may be) with crops, and the ñillatufe scatters grain and asks for abundant harvests. Grains of different sorts have already been placed near the *rewe*. The ñillatufe places handfulls of these grains on the *llupe* (fire), near the main altar. He offers a prayer as the smoke they cause begins to rise toward the sky.

These activities (prayer, in-place dancing, fire offerings) are repeated in the same way as in the first section of the ritual, until the business at hand is completed. The second section of the early morning session ends with a purun around the main altar, after which the participants return to their cooking fires to prepare a midmorning snack. At this time there is a good deal of visiting among the family groups, and guests are given food. Guests are expected to reciprocate these gifts. Indeed, the givers are almost always reciprocating gifts of food they themselves received on another occasion. Also at this time a special kind of sacrifice may be made. This is called *konchotun.*

Konchotun has been discussed by a number of specialists who have written about the Mapuche, and there has been a measure of disagreement with regard to its significance and about the time and manner of its performance. For my part, I have seen konchotun performed several times and in the identical manner. It is a sacrificial act. The sheep (the usual animal employed) may not actually be killed. The participants in the act may simply cut off one of the sheep's ears or merely slice an ear so that blood will flow.

Two men engage in this rite with the rite symbolizing the friendship of the men who conduct it. As indicated previously, these men are usually kinsmen who have a special relationship, perhaps a *vuelta mano* connection, which they wish to emphasize and reinforce in this symbolic manner. The ñillatun fertility ceremony is clearly a most propitious event for such a subsidiary performance.

As mentioned, the agricultural fertility rite usually lasts for two, and sometimes, for three or four days. The second day of the ceremony (and the other days in longer ceremonies) duplicates the first day. The afternoon of the first day duplicates the morning of the first day. The morning of the first day is divided into an early and late session, each of which is identical in basic respects to the other.

There are variations, many due to "sin" or "human frailty." Unplanned variations and unrationalized variations perturb the Mapuche, causing them to perform, sometimes, additional rites. Usually, when it is felt that a ceremonial has been "fouled" by the action of evil beings—blame for this being laid at the feet of the participants in the ceremony—every effort is made to hold a perfect ñillatun the next time. Often "the next time" is after the harvest is in, months after the promissory ñillatun held in anticipation of the harvest. If the harvest is poor, as it is very often, the people feel that they have made errors, committed sins—that the first propitiatory fertility rite was seriously wanting. Therefore, it is customary to hear in the second, and postharvest, ñillatun many expiatory prayers and prayers of thanks for what has been received, thanks to the good offices of the ancestral spirits and the pantheon.

Agricultural fertility rites involve the participation of a number of dominant lineages and their separate reservations (and the subordinate lineages on these). Taken together these reservations may be considered as a ritual congregation. Members of these reservations also form the body of mourners at regional funerals.

To show how this works, let us assume that three reservations form a core unit of ritual responsibility, and call these reservations A, B, and C. As the ritual cycle gets underway, A is the host reservation, during the first year. Its priest-chief (ñillatufe) is the principal official at the ceremony, its officials the leading ones, and so on. Reservations B and C are participants in the ceremony. It is their obligation.

In the following year B is the host reservation and A and C obligatory participants. In the third year it is C's turn; A and B participate. This shared responsibility comes full circle in the fourth year, when A again assumes the position of host group. These three reservations, therefore, constitute a nucleus of responsibility, a center of obligatory ritual participation. In the same general region, however, are other reservations arranged among themselves in a like manner, with small groups of three or four reservations which constitute a nucleus of ritual unities. Some of these reservations, usually those in close physical proximity to the A, B, and C set, are invited to attend the ñillatuns held on A, B, or C. They are invited to participate in a limited way, such as dancing, contributing food, and their attendance is not seen as obligatory; they are invited guests who may refuse to attend if they have other ceremonies to attend.

When these guests from other reservations attend A-B-C ñillatuns regularly, however, and when persons from A-B-C reciprocate by attending regularly the ñillatun on some of these nearby reservations, it is possible to designate this larger ritual grouping as a "ritual congregation." It is also possible to show that this normal assemblage may be designated by a network of matrilateral marriages, the high frequency of which ends at the borders of the ritual congregation.

16

Overview

T HE INTRODUCTION to this case study began with the observation that cultural and social change is an ongoing process, which is related, of course, to cultural and social constancy. This study emphasizes the permanent aspects of Mapuche culture, a perspective often overlooked by anthropologists who concentrate their attention on cultural change.

But cultural and social change are sometimes given little more than passing attention by anthropologists who direct their attention on the functional relationships among social institutions and value systems. There is a sort of makebelieve quality in certain anthropological studies which focus on the supposedly well-integrated social and cultural systems of Tribe X. Although there are good reasons why changes in an over all system (disturbances, perturbations) should be held in their place, while the constant framework is described and analyzed, there are perhaps better reasons for including the perturbations in the description and analysis, when it is possible to do so. Demonstrated change is the measure of cultural and social constancy, the measure of the functional integration of any set of institutions and their ideological framework.

In the colonial setting in which Mapuche society has been viewed, it is, in a sense, appropriate to think of the changes in their traditional way of life as wrought from pressures emanating from outside of their society. Normally, this makes it necessary to consider the impact of Chilean society on the reservation-dwelling Mapuche. But it is descriptively and theoretically wrong to outline these changes by resorting to brief considerations of "modern" items such as plow agriculture, mission schools, and induced needs for kerosene, matches, candles, Western clothing, and so forth. This reduces the Mapuche to an almost mindless population of savages, supporting the common Chilean point of view.

The Mapuche Indians are not well informed about Chilean society, but they are not ignorant. They tend to hang on to the traditional values and institutions they know and feel sure about, and they suspect alien ways of life. This, of course, is not peculiar to the Mapuche, since it is prevalent to all societies, ad-

A Mapuche family, with the author's wife, gather for a fiesta—and their pictures.

vanced or backward. In this latter respect, many of the kinds of adjustments the Mapuche have made in the past 400 years are of more general significance to the understanding of other societies caught up in a colonial situation.

Here we must return to the solid fact of a reservation system which has endured for several generations and which has actually nurtured presentday Mapuche society and helped preserve ageold values which are alien to Spanish-Chilean ways of life. The reservation system provides a fairly stable social setting in which the Mapuche have the opportunity to select, as many societies do, the most effective means of preserving their identity. Social groups can preserve their identity in the face of what appear to be overwhelming odds against their survival.

Only a few Mapuche have made good adjustments to rural and urban Chilean ways of life. But to the vast majority of Mapuche, including those many unfortunates who have tried to make their future in towns and cities of Chile and Argentine, life is grim away from the reservation and, once they have abandoned traditional life for the lure of the cities, life on the reservation is either very uncertain or actually denied them.

The Mapuche—youthful, for the most part—who have abandoned reservation life, number in the thousands, but only about 20- or 30,000 out of a total population of close to 300,000. Mapuche society survives without them. Perhaps reservation society survives because they have left and eased the population pressure on the finite extension of reservation land? The future of Mapuche society does not lie in the cities, an "adjustment" that would destroy their way of life, nor in working for wages for rural Chileans, an accommodation that would demean them, even though they might continue to reside on reservation land. Nonetheless, the Mapuche will have to abandon something, will have to make some accommodation to Chilean desires.

The Mapuche must become educated, not only to the three R's in Spanish, but to the prevailing system of values in Chilean society. How is this to be done in the short time conceived by the action programs of the present government? If "achieved," will the accommodation really be successful? What is going to happen to Mapuche agriculture? This is the main line of advancement of the Chilean reformer. And, then, what changes must take place in the patrilineally based ancestor worship of the Mapuche, with which the agronomist does not concern himself? Do changes in ancestrally based values (antagonistic toward Chilean culture and society) precede worthwhile changes in agricultural techniques, or do changes in the agricultural economy come before changes in the traditional values? Is the modern sharecropping system indicative of change? What is foreboded? Will the Mapuche foresake their ancestral deities and the gods of regional and pan-Mapuche significance, and what might be the result or the conditions of such change?

I do not attempt to answer such questions. I have refrained from asking their full schedule. These are for the reader himself to think about, to discuss, and to decide.

Glossary

AFFINE: Relative by marriage.

admapu: Mapuche customary law.

anchimallen: Small, luminescent ghost.

ARAUCANIAN: The generic term used to designate the Mapuche and their Indian neighbors (the extinct Picunche and the vanishing Huilliche) who speak the language called Araucanian.

awn: Encirclement; funeral ceremony.

chicha: Apple cider, both sweet and fermented, as made by Mapuche and local Chileans.

EXOGAMY: A rule forbidding marriage between members of the same patrilineage.

fundo: A large Chilean farm.

Huilliche: Southern Araucanians.

kalku: Sorcerer-witch.

lonko: Headman of a lineage; chief of a reservation.

machi: Shaman, native curer.

MATRILATERAL MARRIAGE: The customary practice in which a man marries a woman related to him through his mother's "side" of his network of kinsmen; marriage to a *ñuke.*

mingaco: Cooperative labor, involving the participation of a large work gang of of neighbors and kinsmen who are invited to work and are feasted by the host.

ñuke: Kinship term used by a man in reference to any marriageable woman.

ñillatufe: Ritual leader, head of *ñillatun* ceremony.

ñillatun: Agricultural fertility ceremony.

PATRILINEAL DESCENT GROUP: Kinsmen who trace descent through a line of males (agnates) to a common founding ancestor.

PATRILOCALITY: Postmarital residence custom according to which married sons continue to live with their father.

Picunche: Northern Araucanians, now extinct.

pillan: Shaman's familiar spirits; also, god of thunder.

thungulmachin: Shaman's helper.

UXORILOCALITY: Custom according to which a man resides permanently with his wife's parents or other close relatives.

vuelta mano: Reciprocal labor arrangement, often involving two men during their entire mature lifetime.

wekufe: Evil spirits generally.

weupin: Funeral oration and the person who delivers it.

winka: All aliens or non-Mapuche.

witranalwe: A large and ugly ghost.

Yerba maté: Paraguayan tea, a favorite hot drink of Mapuche and rural Chileans.

References

COOPER, FATHER JOHN, 1946, "The Araucanians." *Handbook of South American Indians*, Vol. II, pp. 687–760; Bureau of American Ethnology Bulletin 143, Washington, D.C.

FARON, LOUIS C., 1956, "Araucanian Patri-Organization and the Omaha System." *American Anthropologist*, Vol. LVIII, No. 3, pp. 435–456.

————, 1961, *Mapuche Social Structure: Institutional Reintegration in a Patrilineal Society of Central Chile.* Illinois Studies in Anthropology, No. 1. Urbana: The University of Illinois Press.

————, 1964, *Hawks of The Sun: Mapuche Morality and its Ritual Attributes.* Pittsburgh: University of Pittsburgh Press.

Additional Readings

HILGER, SISTER INEZ, 1957, *Araucanian Child Life and its Cultural Background.* Washington, D.C.: Smithsonian Miscellaneous Collection, Vol. CXXXIII.
Provides information about Chilean *and* Argentine Araucanians.

LATCHAM, RICARDO E., 1909, "Ethnology of the Araucanos." *Journal of the Royal Anthropological Institute*, Vol. XXXIX, pp. 334–370.
First-rate information.

————, 1924, "La organización social y creéncias religiosas de los antiguos araucanos." Santiago, Chile: Imprenta Cervantes.
Despite nineteenth century evolutionary slant, an informative account of the early reservation-period Mapuche.

MCBRIDE, GEORGE MC., 1936, *Chile: Land and Society.* New York: American Geographical Society Research Series, No. 19.
Still one of the best books ever written about rural Chile.

SMITH, EDMOND REUEL, 1855, *The Araucanians.* New York: Harper & Brothers.
Easily read background material of prereservation period Mapuche.

STEWARD, JULIAN, and LOUIS C. FARON, 1959, *Native Peoples of South America.* New York: McGraw-Hill, Inc.
A general coverage of South American indigenous peoples from precolonial times to the present.

TITIEV, MISCHA, 1951, *Araucanian Culture in Transition.* Occasional Contributions, Museum of Anthropology, No. 15. Ann Arbor: The University of Michigan.
The first monograph on the Mapuche by a professional anthropologist.

G   1971